Although born in Scotland, Anna McCabe (until recently) spent most of her life in Wales and England. She returned home in 2017 and now lives in the village of Kincardine with her husband, Peter and their black labrador, Jessie.

A mother of four and Nana to three, Anna teaches English at a secondary school in Fife spending her 'free' time writing, walking, reading, or listening to music.

For Peter, Jack, Rosie, Rhys and Evan, and, for my younger self: Anna the girl.

Anna McCabe

MY TRUTH MIGHT NOT BE YOURS

AUSTIN MACAULEY PUBLISHERS™
LONDON • CAMBRIDGE • NEW YORK • SHARJAH

Copyright © Anna McCabe 2024

The right of Anna McCabe to be identified as author of this work has been asserted by the author in accordance with sections 77 and 78 of the Copyright, Designs and Patents Act 1988.

All rights reserved. No part of this publication may be reproduced, stored in a retrieval system, or transmitted in any form or by any means, electronic, mechanical, photocopying, recording, or otherwise, without the prior permission of the publishers.

Any person who commits any unauthorised act in relation to this publication may be liable to criminal prosecution and civil claims for damages.

The story, experiences, and words are the author's alone.

A CIP catalogue record for this title is available from the British Library.

ISBN 9781035841301 (Paperback)
ISBN 9781035841318 (ePub e-book)

www.austinmacauley.com

First Published 2024
Austin Macauley Publishers Ltd®
1 Canada Square
Canary Wharf
London
E14 5AA

Prologue

4th January 2019, sitting in the lounge of my brother Frank and his wife Beth's house. Frank's not there yet, not back from work, but Beth is. So too is my mum and her husband Alec and next to me, Peter, my husband. Later that day, Peter was to say something to me that would be the inspirational comment I needed to finally put my fingers to keyboard and start this book for the final time. The word in Peter's comment that did it was 'genes'.

Fast forward an hour or so and my niece Lilly comes into the room speaking in a 'highfalutin' accent – quite funny, and definitely something to be commended, not ridiculed as it was. It took me way back, back to my own childhood when anything I did was considered unacceptable and 'different'. Why did it take me back? Because the response to Lilly from Evelyn was, 'You're just like your Aunty Anna, she always wanted to be posh and speak differently to the rest of us.' (Oh, by this time my aunts, Evelyn and Rosemary had arrived). I looked at Evelyn, and unable to remain silent snipped back – 'It was never a case of wanting to be posh or different, it was a case of 'losing' my accent when we moved to Newcastle to stop the bullies from beating me up on a regular basis'. No apology was forthcoming for her cutting remark (as a normal person might expect). No, her response was to note the similarity between my experience and that of her granddaughter who, two years previously, made the journey South with her parents. I am glad I was able to help Evelyn understand a little more of what Simone is going through! My sarcastic thoughts here only serve to show that, although I am different, perhaps not so much. A psychologist might say this internalised sarcasm is a learned coping mechanism; I might be inclined to agree.

Only now, now that Peter's comment has made something click, can I understand that until this year, can I stop observing my life from outside! However, that didn't start until the end of the evening.

#

Back to being a voyeur. I spent the rest of the evening observing my family. In the kitchen, chatting over a bowl of soup, I learnt, (more through her body language than what she says), that Rosemary has been through the most devastating psychological experience she will ever have. I wanted to literally take her by the hand, go somewhere quiet and just hold her, let her talk, let her get it out. But she will never be able to do that, not in this family. Evelyn, at all points, wants to have her voice heard – she has interesting things to say, but it comes out more of a whine than anything else. Not her fault, it is just the way it always has been in this family. Again, this idea of internalising my sarcasm raises its ugly head. I don't dislike Evelyn; in fact, she has at times been like a second mum to me. I have fond memories of childhood evenings spent with her. Some drunken adult ones too! Beth, as always, is a perfect host, but loud – she can't help it either; it's a Scottish thing I'm afraid. You need to raise your voice to be heard. Well, that night, Rosemary didn't raise her voice – but I heard her, I understood her pain … although I'll never be able to tell her that face to face. Why? Because that's just how it is in this family.

#

The night rolled on; more voyeurism only served to reinforce my difference; my distance from the rest of my family members. I watched as my mum and her sisters vied to be the one to talk, to say something funny, or to be heard. I sat, my arms aching, to hold Rosemary, to ease her pain, but still I sat. I'm not so different all the time – I too wanted my voice heard and just occasionally, I managed to get my two-penneth worth in.

Mum and Alec left. I love my mum. Something that people who know me, often ask why, and something you will come to understand as you follow my journey from difference to self-acceptance in the forthcoming pages. I'm my mother's physical double (apart from where we store our fat – that's down to genetics), and we share many of the same quirks. We have both experienced trauma in our lives, alone and together, and just recently, my mum has come to fully understand my life, and I think, me.

Later, Lauren, Beth's friend, sat with me and asked lots of questions about teaching – I'm an English teacher. She was genuinely interested in me, what I do and my perspective on the education system. Not unselfishly, as she has a daughter starting high school in a few months, but nonetheless, ~~I was~~

~~me~~, I was able to feel that I had value in being there. Actually, that's unfair; unfair on my family because they have no idea how I feel. They only see me the way they do because that's how it has always been in this family. Or is it just because I always internalise everything as a coping mechanism, resulting in not being able to express my true self among the very people I should be able to? In reality, it is a bit of both.

All the time, I'm observing everything going on around me (as always) and note that Frank is relatively quiet. Perhaps he's a bit more like me than I thought, biding his time before saying anything, but then, he too has been through trauma. Something I know that everyone in the room has been through too. Maybe that's the difference my genetics gives me; the capacity to be different despite life.

The evening ends and we drive home. I'm quiet as we start off and Peter is not oblivious to this. I can feel the air full of particles; particles of my mind floating, wanting to know what makes me different. So, because I know he will know the answer, I ask him why.

#

'It's in your genes. Your dad was different than anyone on this side of your genetic family, and your sisters are all different. Like you, they have degrees, are professional women and hold a completely different perspective on life.'

#

A little explanation: my biological father never wanted anything to do with me and just four years ago, I was finally able to trace that side of my family. I discovered he had died of a heart attack in 1991 and that I have three half-sisters and a half-brother (he died at a few days old).

#

So now you have a choice – decide that you need to know no more about my journey through a life of being different and put this book to the side, or turn the page and join me, because I am now going to take the self-same journey with you. Except this time, I will be viewing it from a different perspective.

Sausages

#

Sausages, I know! What a title for the opening chapter of a novel about a personal journey searching for self-acceptance! Well, I hope by the end of the following pages, you will understand why I thought this a good place to start.

#

My earliest memory is of lying on the sofa with my grandfather. It was New Year's Day. I can't remember how old I was, but I do know that I hadn't started school, and I now know that by the end of that day, in my small child's mind, I was different! The fire wasn't lit, so there was a blanket over me and Grandad. It was relatively early in the day, so I was still in my nightdress. What followed over the following few minutes is fully ingrained in my mind … Grandad put one of his sausage-shaped fingers inside my privates. Shocked? I wasn't because I knew no better. I thought this is what happens when you cuddle up with your Grandfather.

#

Somewhere deep inside my little girl's head, I knew I was not allowed to speak about this – Granddad never told me not to (not like Henry – more on that later), but I just knew. This is what made me different, even at such a young age – certainly not older than 4 years old – I responded to a situation in the opposite manner to what one might expect. I mean, I'm sure if I'd asked my mum why Granddad put his fingers inside me, she would have responded appropriately. Although, in hindsight, I'm not sure she would have. Not because she wasn't a good mother, but because in the early 70s, sexual abuse of a child was very rarely talked about; it was the forbidden taboo.

Fast forward to my latest, and most successful therapy: Art therapy. In my current school, we have a woman, Jenny, who supports our young people, and when I was speaking to another teacher, it was suggested that Jenny may be able to help with my self-esteem. So, I thought why not – asking Jenny for help has been my turning point. During the first few sessions, Jenny gave me a focus for my drawings – a tree, a person, and then a house. After these, I would just draw and talk. I am no artist! Jenny would ask questions and really importantly for me, they were in the third person. For example, 'How did Anna feel when …'. This allowed me to be more objective, to think about my experiences as an adult and to both analyse and evaluate my own response to the trauma I experienced.

The following drawing from this therapy provides a timely discussion point.

This drawing is from session 5. Whenever I started my 'free' drawing, I always started with a curved line. It just felt natural, and from this, I would build my drawing. I didn't think about it, I just did it. The man above is my Grandfather. I started with the line of his hat (1). I remember drawing the hat and realising it looked like a sailor's hat – well, to me it did anyway. Grandad was in the Navy during WWII. Jenny asked me about him, though I can't remember the specifics, but I do remember the focus of this session ended up being about my relationship with my grandparents and food.

The building is a block of four flats, with Gran's in the top right (2). Actually, there were three rows of flats and Gran's was in the middle. I spent a lot of time there, not all of it bad. I loved walking to Gran's at lunchtime when I was at school to walk their dog, 'Max.' Once we'd walked, I'd put Dolly

Parton's 'Coat of Many Colours' on the turntable and wrap my arms around Max. I was safe. I was warm. I was loved.

This session highlighted that Grandad's hands held fear for me, (note the sausage/weapon-like appearance of them). His menacing eyes and the fact that he is so dark just serves to emphasise the fact I have no good feelings about him – none! You would think that I would feel cheated; I don't. I only feel indifference whenever I think of him, or anyone mentions him.

Back to my session 5 drawing, the 'plan' is a rough sketch of Gran's flat.

a) balcony
b) lounge
c) Rosemary's room
d) Gran and Grandad's room
e) bathroom
f) kitchen
g) cupboard

In that cupboard was a cake. My Aunt Pippa's wedding cake (or the part that was being saved for when the first baby might come along). Whenever I was at Gran's, I would steal into the cupboard and take a bit of the cake. I couldn't resist it. I also couldn't understand that I was stealing. I wasn't hungry – I just wanted it. No, I would go so far as to say I needed it. Those bits of stolen cake made me feel good. I strongly believe that this was the beginning of my destructive relationship with food. Even now, I will eat in secret. I'll go to the shop and take the long way back so I can stuff my face and dispose of the evidence.

There's no fooling Peter (or the scales though). I am slowly working on this now as my health has suffered. Can I blame this on the abuse I endured? Partly – it is certainly where it began. Now though, it is only me abusing my body (out of habit) and this is a habit which needs to be broken.

When Gran questioned me about the cake, I couldn't lie – I have one of those faces, definitely not a poker face. She was mad, so very mad at me. She shouted and screamed at me. I have no recollection of her words apart from the swearing and being called a thief as well as a liar. Our relationship never recovered from 'Cake Gate.' I can't remember if she told Mum, but when she and I discussed it recently, Mum had no recollection. More importantly for me, Mum told me that if she had, she would have given Gran a piece of her mind for speaking to me like that.

I remember reading some wise words once, though where I do not know, these words essentially put forward the idea that when we talk about things that happen to us or we are involved in then our version becomes our truth. More importantly, I recall words to the effect that if repeated often enough the events themselves become a reality in the minds of ourselves and those around us.

#

These words ring true with me because as I grew up my grandmother labeled me a liar. As a consequence of this, I continually questioned myself, my memories and my feelings. I also know that there are things that I have made up that have become 'truths'. These same truths are the things that I felt made me interesting. Though I know now that all they were, was a way of covering up the real truth – 'I am different'. I was being abused and thought it was 'my' normal, but I wanted it to be everybody else's normal!

Perhaps a prime example of just how my gran viewed my value was when, one boxing day, (or very close to it) our house set on fire. It was mid-afternoon. My baby brother was asleep on the sofa and we were all just in that post-Christmas slump. Mum went out to the loo and discovered the smoke. Calmly, she instructed me to go to Gran's and let her know. I will never forget this moment. It was a month before my sixth birthday, and I ran pell-mell from our house to Gran's. I remember my chest burning, and the sweat pouring down my face. When I got there, Gran was scrubbing the stairs (you don't see people doing that now) and the conversation went something like this:

#

A: Gran, Gran our house is on fire.
Gran: Stop your lying, of course it's not on fire, you're just wanting attention.
A: No Gran, I swear, it's on fire. Mum sent me to get you.
Gran: Stop it, Anna. I don't need to hear your tall tales, I'm busy ...

#

Cue the sirens and she finally believed me. Did I get an apology? Of course I didn't – I never did.

Going back to the words from earlier – they might not be exactly as spoken, but the gist is there, and this is one of my 'real truths.' I don't want to confuse you as you read, so if something I mention is not a real 'truth,' I will make sure it is obvious.

I often wonder if my gran's belief that I was a liar meant she knew what was going on and that if I was a liar no one would believe me if I ever did speak up. As well as Max, Dolly Parton and 'Cake Gate', I have strong memories of being at their flat, my brothers with me, Gran working away in the kitchen and Granddad laying me on their old bed. He would put me on my back with my bottom resting on the hard wooden foot rail and perform oral sex on me. Just the thought of it now gives me the creeps – I wasn't even 9!

Inside my stomach would be churning because if Gran walked in, I'd be in trouble. I had absolutely no notion that I was innocent in all of this.

#

Apart from this, my early childhood was unremarkable. I had friends who I fought with (that's what little girls do). I also had male friends whom I played with (that's what this little girl did). I always was a bit of a tomboy. I enjoyed climbing trees and playing Cowboys and Indians. I was even pretty good at getting my brothers into trouble. Once, I let the handbrake off of Dad's van, which then gently rolled into someone's garage. Quick as a flash, I grabbed my little brother (who couldn't really speak then) and put him in the driver's seat. Think I was in my 40s before I owned up to that one! Actually, maybe I still haven't, to be honest, I can't remember.

#

Recently, I visited Frank and his family, and ironically this very subject came up. So, I sat down to do an edit before writing further and immediately came to this point to put the matter straight. I mentioned earlier the wise words regarding how our own truths become a reality if repeated often enough, and I made a promise that I would ensure that the things I thought were my truths but might not be true at all would be obvious. Frank's face when I told him what I thought happened struck to my core. Thinking about it, I realised that at that moment, I possibly shattered a memory for him with something that I had claimed for myself, just so I could fit in. The result is this – I know the event happened, but in reality, I don't know if I had anything to do with it. Was I just there to witness it? I hope Frank can forgive me or at the very least understand why my traumatised brain might mold the truth to create a 'normality' for me in an otherwise abnormal childhood.

#

My life began to change when we moved from that house to one just a few streets away. The family next door were good fun and my brothers and I enjoyed going to the local fields and jumping from small cliffs onto hay bales. We did all the normal stuff pre-teens do (I was the only female). There was a park directly outside our door where I spent many an hour sitting on the swings just thinking. Being alone. Being me.

It was around this time that I think I started to know that what was happening to me was not right and that I was not at fault. But, and this is a big BUT, I also knew that I couldn't ask for help. Partly because in 1978, abuse 'didn't happen', and also because I was a liar not to be believed. I was very good at making up stories. I had a great imagination. In essence, I believe I was conditioned into protecting my abusers from a very early age.

#

One of the telltale signs of sexual abuse is promiscuity – yep, that was me.

Granddad caught me in bed with the next-door neighbour (I was 10 – he was 13) experimenting. We were both fully dressed, though he did have his 'willy' out which I remember was very small. Granddad went ballistic. I got into so much trouble for that and was never allowed to be on my own with my neighbour ever again. Hypocrite! Actually, putting this on paper has allowed me to look at the experience objectively, and in all honesty, this memory is quite funny. It is also the sort of memory many 'non-abused' people will have because it is perfectly normal to experiment sexually (just not quite so young).

#

The real change came the Christmas before my 11th birthday. Boxing day, Mum had left me and my brothers with (our sleeping) dad while she went to see my grandparents, as Gran had had an operation a few weeks earlier – for some reason, she said not to tell him where she was. When Dad woke up, he was furious. He wanted to know where she had gone and I wouldn't tell him. He got really mad; he began hitting me so I ran next door only to be dragged back by my hair. He kept slapping me and I remember my head hitting the wall – it was that bumpy stuff – and feeling the little cuts on my face. Finally, Rob (my older brother) made me tell him. So, Dad marched us up to our grandparents' house, told my mother he was leaving her and stormed out. Rob then blurted out what Dad had done to me and Granddad went running out after him as if to give him a taste of his own medicine.

My most memorable moment of that day is not my dad's anger and treatment of me, it was thinking that my Grandfather was so two-faced – a wolf in sheep's clothing – I would say now as an adult. He spouted something along the lines that no one got to hurt his granddaughter and get away with it. He got away with hurting me though. The only positive comment I could ever pass about him is that my grandfather never got me to do anything to him. I never saw his penis or saw him perform any sexual act on himself.

#

I feel here that I need to further explain my parentage – my dad is not my biological father. My mother had a bit of a rubbish time with men and her first husband (Rob's biological father) was violent. In between him and Dad, Mum met my biological father and only found out that he was married when I was three weeks old. Despite his violence (very rare), I always felt that Dad WAS my dad. I have so many fond memories of the times spent with him. I learned how to look after my bike from him, how to carry out household chores, and how to work effectively in the garden. He took me to events such as fetes where Batman and Robin were there with their car. During my childhood years, he was the only adult male in my life who treated me the way a father should. He was my dad.

The above is my drawing from session 3, Jenny asked me to draw a house.

Without any thought, I went straight to drawing the house in Valley Gardens, although looking at it now, the lower floor needs swapping as the lounge window (the bigger one) was to the right of the door as you look at it. All those good things about my dad are represented in this drawing.

1) The shed where we would spend hours making things (woodwork, etc). I was banned from the shed in Cheviot Road for a few weeks before one Christmas while Dad secretly built me a doll's house. I can still see it in my mind's eye now – wallpaper and all.
2) My bike, upside down, while he taught me how to repair it.
3) The sieve he'd get me to use while prepping soil. The star – he dug and I helped him plant in the front garden.
4) My bedroom, exactly how it was laid out. Painted a beautiful primrose yellow and my quilt cover (pink with yellow flowers)

All of these memories are great, warm and fond. Parts of my childhood I love to dwell on.

#

After Dad left, life for me changed forever as Mum moved Henry in. I had met him previously in town as Mum felt she could trust me and took me to have pancakes with him. I had my ears pierced that day – something Dad said I couldn't have done till I was 16.

As an adult now looking back, it is quite clear that the ear piercing was a deliberate two-finger salute to my dad, but also a clear indicator of Henry's intent. Having read several articles/books on the subject, it is routine for abusers to isolate the intended target early on and by getting Mum to introduce me to him first (for it was his idea of that I am sure) he set his dastardly plan in action.

#

Now, he was living with us.

Bath

#

Sunday night – bath night! I loved bath nights before Henry arrived. It was always just us as a family in the house (no Grandad). Then Henry was living with us. For some reason I can't remember, Mum was not at home that night. I remember having my bath and making sure the door to the bathroom was locked because HE was there and I felt uneasy.

Besides, lying in the bath was always my own time; a time when no one could hurt me, a time where I could think and put everything into perspective. I clearly recall those moments; the thoughts running through my head would go something like this:

So, this week, I've managed to avoid seeing him (Granddad) three times. When I was there, I was able to not 'sleep with him' by pretending I had homework to do – his face was a picture. He knew I was deliberately avoiding giving him 'cuddles.' He is a dirty, shitty bastard and doesn't deserve to live. One day, he will have a long painful death and I will sit next to his bed feeling smug because he will be suffering. Right, let's put him in his box and think about all the good things about this week ….

#

Clearly, the above is a precis of what I thought, and perhaps I didn't use those exact sentences (but I did call him a dirty, shitty bastard daily) and equally clearly at the age of 11, I was consciously talking to myself about my experiences and using strategies to deal with them. Today, this has a term – positive self-talk. I did get to sit next to his bed when he was dying of prostate cancer, and I do know he was in pain. Mum asked me to speak to the doctors as I worked for a health authority at the time and therefore, would know what they were talking about. As it happened, I did, and the words palliative care relayed have stuck in my head from that day. He was going to be cared for while he was dying, and even though a small voice inside wanted to scream and shout, 'No, the bastard deserves no such thing,' I knew I was wrong.

Even predators deserve some dignity in their passing.

However, I digress … what followed that particular bath would put an end to it being my positive space. When I was dried, dressed in my thick jimjams and wrapped in my dressing gown, I went into the living room where the fire was on higher than usual. It was bloody hot in there! Now you tell me, what is it about a prepubescent girl, completely trussed up in childish nightwear with soaking wet hair that arouses a grown man? The answer should be nothing. Henry was not a man, he was a complete and utter misbegotten mongrel. I dearly wish I had a wider vocabulary then – I would have been able to ridicule him and he wouldn't have known what I was saying because he was such a moronic being.

The eagle-eyed reader will have noted at the end of the previous chapter no mention was made of the number 5 element of my session 3 drawing. A deliberate action on my part as that is a depiction of the night Henry claimed me as his object of desire. This is the lounge in Valley Gardens showing Henry on a chair next to the fire and me face down on the sofa. Above the number 5 are two boxes; on the left is the bathroom, the right is the kitchen.

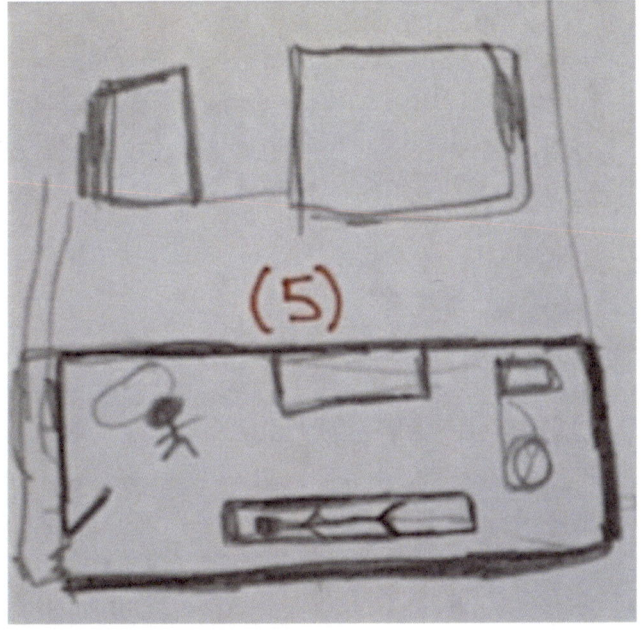

Henry grabbed my hand as I entered the room and pulled me onto his knee. He 'cuddled' me and whispered in my ear – 'isn't this nice.' I didn't answer. I just froze. This is a natural response to danger and usually comes before or after the flight or fight response. I couldn't fight nor could I flee, therefore my only option was to freeze, putting me at the mercy of the danger which threatened me – HIM! After a few minutes, he let me go and I attempted to flee. I started towards the door, but from behind me, Henry's deep voice 'suggested' that I lie down on the sofa. I remember being brave and taking another step forward before he repeated his suggestion, only this time there was something in the way he uttered the words that stopped my heart and sent shivers of ice through my blood. Looking back at this precise moment, I know this is when I became detached from everyone and everything. Even now as an adult, I have to consciously be present in the lives of those I know and love. While some might suggest that this means I am damaged, I would argue that actually we are all created by our environment and I would not be able to love at all if I had not been strong enough to survive that particular period of my life using this strategy.

#

I did as suggested – but I lay on my front. At the time I just did this and never knew why, but I believe not being able to see him somehow stopped it being real. Lying there was torture, it was so hot I wanted to remove my dressing gown but also didn't want to remove it. Then he told me to, so I did. Henry took hold of my hair, laid it down my back and proceeded to brush it. All the time, his hand was firmly placed on my butt cheek. In my readings, one thing that recurs is the idea that paedophiles truly believe they are doing nothing wrong, even though they know society sees their actions as morally reprehensible and illegal, they simply see themselves as natural. Hence, when I look back at this moment, I can see how he would have explained this to my mother should she have walked in, and in those days, there would not even have been a hesitation to think that the situation wasn't anything other than what he said.

#

Lying in bed that night all my insides felt so heavy that I believed I could simply just fall to the centre of the earth. I can now identify this sensation as one of utter and total despair – I had two male adults who were meant to look after me, to guide me safely through my youth and protect me from the dangers that lurked in the world doing the exact opposite.

Even though I knew that I was not at fault, that they were both wrong, I still kept it inside.

The fact that they were predators and I their prey somehow felt my burden to carry. I believed that everywhere I went, people looked at me and saw a misfit, someone to be used and not regarded as of any worth. I would walk down the street and see other kids my age engaging in a genuine manner with their adults and wonder what it would be like to be them, to be able to do everyday things as a child should – without a care in the world.

I know that some of these children were in the same, if not worse position than I was. I also know that this is one reason why I don't judge the children I teach on their behaviour. I see them as humans going through their education with an external life that I have little to no knowledge of. I don't assume they are lazy, rude, disrespectful and aggressive – these are just behaviours. I aim to teach with empathy and compassion. Mostly I get it right. Sometimes, I don't, and it is at these points that I learn.

The Move

#

My last year at Valley Primary School was coming to an end. We were taken on our transition day visit to High School – Kirkcaldy High. I remember it was the old building, (which has now been replaced with some swanky new houses). The green corridors were very hospital-like. I walked those corridors with my classmates, but I was alone. I spoke to no one; I had no close friends. Looking back, it is clear that this was another coping strategy. If I didn't have friends then they wouldn't be able to identify what it was about me that was wrong, what was different. Kirkcaldy High seemed like a place where I could become someone, where I could just work away quietly and begin the journey towards adulthood. My cousins were there and my older brother too – I'd have people to look out for me. No … Henry had other ideas and we made a move.

#

During the long summer holiday, we moved to Methil, some 8 ½ miles from my home town of Kirkcaldy. The reason for the move; they were to become publicans. Their first foray into this new world was a large hotel which stood on the top of a hill. The building overlooked the rig building yards on the edge of the Firth of Forth, quite an astonishing view.

It was fascinating to watch as the oil rigs developed from just legs to legs with platforms. The daily difference was minute, but over time, those little differences grew into a much larger and complete structure. Quite an apt metaphor for the development of the human psyche, where all external influences have a role to play in the overall structure of us as human beings. But it is how we, the original, deal with those external influences that really cement the structure together. Henry had a huge external influence on me, and even though this influence remains part of my psyche today, it is how I have dealt with it and other influences which have turned me into the human being I am today.

Becoming publicans and moving away was the next step in Henry's plan to isolate his targets (for my mum was one too). He got us away from the eyes of our immediate family. He then set about alienating my younger brother by accusing him of stealing from the bar, etc. Long story short, my dad got custody of Frank – the best thing that could possibly have happened to him. Not for Mum, but for Frank. Of the three of us, Frank went on to have, what could be termed, a normal childhood and progression into adulthood. This is something I am very grateful for. My older brother and I were stuck. Dad had been in the process of officially adopting us, but it was not complete, so he had no 'claim' to us. Years later when he 'found out', he broke down in tears and bemoaned the fact that I had not told him as '[he] would've found a way.' A nice thought, but I know I wouldn't have left my mum – as an adult

I know why back then, I just knew I had to stay with her, no matter what.

Just like the rigs changed little by little, so too did I. I had already and would continue to change internally, and Henry ensured that I would also change externally in a way that subtly announced his possession of me. With the move to Methil, I would be attending a new school, Kirkland High. Three days before term, Mum, Rob and I walked to Leven. As we were passing a park (in which there was a pony with a very big penis – strange the things you remember), Mum informed us that our surname was now 'Campbell' – Henry's name. We had no say in the matter; we just had to accept it. They weren't married, but it appeared he had persuaded Mum that we should be seen as a 'proper' family from the get-go. So I started Kirkland High as Jane Campbell. I spent nearly three years at Kirkland and have some happy memories of my time there.

#

I met my first proper boyfriend there – Malcolm Bryant – he was in the year above me. Malcolm made me feel good – he held me with very strong arms. To this day, I can still feel those arms and how safe I felt when I was in them. Malcolm played the trombone, and I the cornet. We both played for the Buckhaven High School Orchestra (Kirkland's arch-enemy) and The Buckhaven and Methil Borough Brass Band. I will treasure forever the trip we made with the orchestra to Sweden. We were there for a week, during which time we played at many venues, however, Malcolm and I spent every spare moment together.

I look so happy and carefree in this photo with Malcolm as he proved he could carry me around in his arms. I WAS safe, I didn't just feel safe.

#

Staying with my musical exploits. There were trips to Blackpool with the brass band for the annual championships. These should have been times of joy for me, but the knowledge of what I was returning to just made them pass too quickly. Henry was exceptionally jealous, yes, I said, jealous. You see, like many paedophiles, he truly believed that he was 'in a relationship with me' and as a result, I dreaded returning after any trip as I would be faced with the 'deviant inquisition' and he never believed a word I said. The only way to protect myself was to ensure that I didn't do anything wrong, that way I couldn't lie. Despite my gran's belief, I wasn't a very good liar. That didn't stop him from terrorising me, constantly trying to 'catch me out' so that he would have something to hold over me. I was in a permanent state of heightened awareness. Continually aware of where he was physically, reading his moods, assessing his level of alcohol intake – I was a young girl, I should have been carefree, but I wasn't.

The days at the White Swan hold only darkness for me. I have absolutely no happy memories of that building in any way, shape or form. I still have nightmares about it; the stairs going down to the back of the building are stairs I quite often descend in my dreams – never reaching the bottom. However, it was not those stairs that held my stomach in knots, even now, almost 42 years later. I can't remember exactly when, but it was not long after we moved there so I was definitely 12 when Henry came up to the residents' lounge (somewhere he must have known I was hiding from him) and took me by the hand. He walked me along the corridor – now, I've never watched the film Psycho, but I've seen clips and this memory makes me think of that film every single time! The main corridor was quite grand – along the middle ran a red carpet with the polished oak floor visible on either side so that the carpet almost had the impression of a runway. With the resident's lounge at my back, there were several doors on either side. Six of these were 'resident's rooms', one was the resident's bathroom, and another was ours. At the other end (the end nearest to Leven), there were the doors of our quarters. About halfway on the left-hand side, there was a door which led to the attic. This is where he was taking me.

#

I watched as his hand opened the door. He looked to see that no one was around and pushed me through. He made me climb the stairs, his hand on my bottom as he did so. Now, I had been up there before – hiding – this time though, there was no feeling of safety. The dust on the stairs rose in little spirals of air as we ascended into the attic room. An attic room reminiscent of many old black and white films where the mad wife is locked away. This one was dusty, to the point that sneezing was inevitable. The small circular window was broken and pigeons had used the room frequently as their bathroom. The smell was cloying, a mixture of dirt and bird excrement struck me as usual, only this time it made me want to vomit, but I didn't. This was the day that marked my real entrance to the world of adult sexual activity; this was the day that my mind created its safe place.

#

Henry was wearing his usual nylon trousers, grey if I remember correctly. When we got into the room, he got his penis out. It soon became erect – he took my hand and put it around his penis and told me what to do. I don't think it took long. I do remember him getting angry because I wasn't holding it hard enough or moving fast enough. I also remember thinking, why am I doing this? How long will this take? Then he started to make these stupidly weird noises and he ejaculated. This was my first ever experience with semen, mixed with the dust and pigeon excrement, the smell was absolutely horrid. This smell lives with me still. I can remember precisely my actions which followed. I turned to my left and wiped my hands on the dusty wall to remove what I could. I then ran down the stairs to the bathroom and washed my hands vigorously before returning to the residents' lounge. There are images that stick and along with those images, one can hold the emotions experienced; this is one of those occasions. When I returned to the residents' lounge, I picked up my book and continued reading as if nothing had happened. I felt empty, hollow like a barrel that just exists to stand in the corner of a cellar and fill space. Looking back now, I am fully aware that my mind was creating boxes to hold those memories and keep them away from my immediate consciousness. Earlier, I talked about becoming detached from everyone and everything, but at this precise moment, I also think I became detached from my own life. Even today, I sometimes feel detached.

The Stalker

#

Henry was all about control; he controlled my life entirely. I have a variety of memories which can testify to how he controlled me through fear. Putting his hand up my skirt in public is one. Making me believe no one would believe me if I spoke up was another – they all do that! Looking at it now, I wonder how many people saw these signs, the other kids behind me as he put his hand on my backside and squeezed when I was getting on a bus for a trip with the Swedish orchestra when they came to Scotland, sitting too close to me when we went out, jumping away from me when they walked into a room. Of course they saw, but it was the forbidden taboo, nothing like that could happen in their life to someone they knew/loved.

When the Swedish orchestra visited Scotland, I was no longer with Malcolm. I got very close to one of their members – Per Ola Nielson. He was six foot tall, blonde and very, very good-looking. We 'hitched up' for the duration of their trip, just a week, but a week with some good memories. Of course, Henry spoiled that too.

#

Firstly, the girl who had been housed with me was moved to another family after the first night. We were not told specifically why, but it was clear she felt threatened. The night of the day they arrived, Henry was his usual argumentative self. He became abusive verbally to both me and my mother in front of this girl and even when I had removed her from the situation, he carried on shouting obscenities at my mother. She couldn't look me in the eye the rest of the week. As an adult now, I think it might have been more than Henry's vocal abuse – otherwise, she might have talked about it and made fun of me the way teenagers do. But in hindsight, it is clear that he tried something with her and she, unlike me, had a get-out.

#

Towards the end of the week, we had a barbecue on Leven Beach. Per Ola and I were sitting around the fire with everyone else, just cuddling and keeping warm. There was alcohol there, but I was not drinking. I looked up and saw some car headlights – ten minutes later and they were still there. It was too dark to make out the car, but I knew it was him. Per Ola and I moved away from the group. We were just chatting when 'he' came out of nowhere and dragged me away. When I say dragged, I mean dragged. Per Ola, poor bloke, just stood and stared after us wondering what was happening.

When they had gone home, Per Ola and I wrote to one another for about six months. One day though, I received a letter where he talked about finding someone else and didn't find it right to keep up our correspondence. He used the words (and I do remember these very clearly) 'Just ask your father how hard it is to love two women at the same time'.

Per Ola obviously was referring to what he saw as Henry's 'love' for me as a daughter. How close yet far away from the truth he was.

#

Stalking became Henry's second favourite pastime. Whenever I did go out with friends, he would be there, sitting in his car, watching. I would go to the cinema only to come out and he'd be there. Anywhere I went, where there was any possibility of me spending time with a boy, he was there! How my mother never suspected I'll never know and while I do not hold any of this against her, I do feel she should have done more to protect me. I know if I suspected anyone was behaving in any way unusual towards my kids, I would have at least made investigations, (probably with my past), and I would have walked away with my kids.

The above snip comes from the drawing I did in my second session with Jenny, she asked me to draw a person, which will be discussed later. But for now, the above section clearly conveys just how much I felt 'watched' (it was highly intimidating as indicated by the size of the eyes in relation to Henry and the car). There would always be a knot in my stomach whenever I went out; I'd constantly be looking over my shoulder for the car headlights. Initially, Henry stayed at a reasonable distance, but it was not long before he was so close we could smell the smoke from his cigarettes wafting from the open car window. It's quite funny that today, my friends would very quickly tell their parents about my stalker and those parents would do something about it. Then though, in the early 1980s, people turned a blind eye. In that respect, society has improved, to a certain extent, in that people are much more aware and sensitive to the evil that surrounds us.

If I were a teenager today, I'd like to think that I would get the help I so badly wanted and needed back then.

While we lived in Methil, I would occasionally spend the weekend back in Kirkcaldy at my Grandparents'. Yes, I know – why? Well, to be honest, my time there was easier and less traumatic than at the hotel. I used to go on the bus and return the same way. That bus journey is one that I can recall quite readily at any time. The houses we would pass, the graveyard, the villages – all things that could not hurt me and a time when I could just be free from threat. You see, I do have some positive memories and this bus journey is up there among them. I would sit on the top deck and watch the countryside pass me by, thinking about anything and everything, just enjoying being on my own. No dirty man putting his hands up my skirt or putting my hand down his trousers. Just me, my mind and a packet of midget gems.

#

One weekend, however, Henry came to Kirkcaldy to fetch me. I can't remember what kind of car it was, in fact, I remember nothing about it at all. I do remember getting to the Standing Stones road and he pulled over next to a wood. I remember him taking me into that wood, and I remember him ejaculating in that wood – that is all! The box in which this memory is stored is firmly closed. Part of me wants to get it out and deal with it, but a great part of me is terrified of what the box might contain. I do know that I can't walk in woods when the acorns have dropped as it makes me feel physically sick and I have a very, very strong physical reaction to anything that is full of holes or bumps. As a rational adult, I know that these things can't harm me and perhaps, one day, I will look into the EMDR therapy that was mentioned to me recently.

#

After 2 years in Methil, my weekends of semi-freedom ended when we made another move; a much bigger one this time. Life was about to get even worse for me…

Gateshead

#

I remember my last parent's evening at Kirkland High very clearly. All my teachers were optimistic that I was capable of obtaining 8 O'levels; in particular, my French teacher said I was a 'natural'. However, all this was to become a 'lie' as a result of the next stage of Henry's sick plan for my future. As I've mentioned a couple of times, I have read a lot about abusers. I have also explained how their first act is to isolate their targets. Well, Henry took this a step further and just as I was coming to the end of S3, we moved away again. This time, we moved to Felling in Gateshead, Tyne and Wear. I will never forget that pub and its layout on all three levels.

Then there was the pub itself – a long building with doors at either end. The smell of stale beer and cigarettes lives on in my memory. When the cleaners were in, I did like the smell of disinfectant, furniture polish and brasso. When the pub was open and I was on this level, I was relatively safe. He'd still be quite harsh with his words, but at least I was physically safe.

Our quarters on the top floor holds nothing but turmoil in my brain. At one end of the bar, there was a door through to the toilets, and through that, the first door led upstairs to our 'home'. To the left at the top of the stairs was the kitchen, and to the right, another step which took you into the rest of the flat. The flat ran the length of the pub with three bedrooms on the left, a bathroom in the middle on the right and a large lounge at the end which was the width of the building.

Mum and Henry had the first room, me the second and Rob the one closest to the lounge. My room was quite large; there were two windows in it, two single beds, a wardrobe and a bed settee. The rest of my schooling took place while we lived there and I left Heworth Grange Comprehensive with no O'levels only CSEs and poor grades in those too. At the time, when I was struggling to retain information to get good marks on tests, etc., I tried to study but just couldn't concentrate. I was also mentally drained from the constant fear of Henry, of my mum finding out and of getting into trouble that I'm not surprised I didn't succeed academically. At the time, I thought that my gran was right, that I was thick and would never amount to anything. Now though, I know differently. I know that my young brain couldn't cope with protecting myself from the effects of the abuse and learning at the same time. As a teacher, I can have an educated guess at the kind of comments my own teachers may have made: 'She's always quiet', 'no trouble', 'just sits and gets on with her work.' I was one of the kids who 'flew under the radar'. I didn't want to bring attention to myself because if I did, they might see how 'bad' I was. I was relatively happy at school. I had some friends and I was safe while I was there. So safe, that even when I was ill, I wouldn't say anything, just so I could be at school.

On one occasion, I had a period from hell (I was about 15). I remember sitting in the common room with my head out the window for fresh air. My form teacher – Mr Johns – came walking across the schoolyard and two minutes later, I heard him talking to my head of house (she was a right bitch, can't remember her name, just her acerbic tongue). Next thing I know, he walks into the common room and picks me up – yes, picks me up. He carries me across the schoolyard to his car and drives me home. I can still remember the mixed feelings I had that day; firstly, gratitude to this man who was both my form tutor and my history teacher and who was treating me with such care and respect, but also some anger that I would have to spend more time at home than necessary. I often think about Mr Johns and the effect he had on me. In today's world, he would have been the teacher I disclosed to – I know he would have ensured that the correct procedures were followed. But we all know that in those days, I was the liar. More importantly, I know from the following years that Henry would get away with it.

As well as my inability to achieve academically at that time, there were also many other areas where I missed out – something which came up in my second session with Jenny.

In the last chapter, there was a snippet from this drawing from session 2. I was asked to draw a person. I drew several! I started with me in the middle and then Dan on my right. I then drew the car on the right of the paper (not very accurate but it was a red estate). To begin with, in this session, I was reasonably happy and calm, but as I continued to draw and got to the part with Henry's eyes, my anger started to bubble inside me. It was because of the impact Henry had on my relationships that I became angry in this session. Anger you can clearly see in my depiction of Henry in the bottom right with a 'dick' on his face – he was a total dickhead. We gave my drawings titles and this one is titled 'Lost Chances', highlighting the sadness I feel when I think about the fact that I never got to experience a natural teenage romance, not fully anyway.

The one that hurts the most is Dan. He was the 'non-cool' cool kid at school, always wearing very tight cord trousers which were not the school uniform and weren't even of the same colour as the uniform. We were inseparable at school, but outside of school, we struggled to see each other without Henry turning up in his red estate car, watching like a vulture ready to pounce as soon as we even came into contact. He didn't pounce though and I got a little braver – a bravery I would always pay for when I went home. This was usually in the form of very loud verbal abuse – the violence didn't really start until later.

Dan and I went steady for about 4 months – we were good together. We enjoyed walks, and talking about anything and everything. We kissed, we held hands and genuinely took pleasure in each other's company. This, I'm afraid, was as far as it went, all because of Henry and his controlling behaviour. We had to part.

All of the other kids in the drawing are representative of other pupils at the school – I didn't make friends easily because I didn't really want to take them home. This gave the impression that I was aloof and resulted in some heavy bullying (I couldn't win either way). My detachment today could also be seen as being aloof, and I still struggle to make friends. This I find quite annoying because Henry is no longer around and hasn't been anywhere near me for 28 years, so why am I still this way? Clearly, the behaviours we adopt in childhood are very hard to dispense with as adults.

Hell on Earth

\#

I have given this chapter this title purely because my time in Gateshead was when the abuse became worse. We lived in other places where the abuse was even worse, but this is the place where the 'hard stuff' began.

\#

With my love of music, you would have thought that I would join an orchestra or a brass band – no – I decided to stay clear, not because I didn't love playing my instrument, or the sense of belonging this would give me. I didn't join either because I couldn't face the embarrassment I had in the past. What should have given me joy and peace would only bring another level of stress to my life. Just another example of how I was being isolated.

\#

I do remember the first time I played at school – the teacher asked me to play something so he could see what level I was at. I stood up and without music, played Puppet on a

String – great for the full range of musical notes. He was stunned and from that day forward, I would help him with other students because he had only just started the brass section in school.

#

I have a very strange memory from my time at Heworth Grange. We put on the play, 'Joseph and his multi-coloured coat'. It was fantastic. We had some brilliant singers in our year group and some really good musicians. I offered to be part of the orchestra pit but they didn't have any other brass instruments in there and the teacher said I would have to transpose the entire musical script for my cornet to fit in. I said I would really love to do that. Ultimately though, I was unable to because, by this time, Henry was doing everything to stop me from being able to spend time on things I enjoyed. However, the play was a time for me to get away. So, for five nights, I sat in that orchestra pit with my cornet to my lips playing the occasional note to 'enhance' the music! In reality, I added nothing but I did get myself several Henry free hours more than usual.

#

Another thing I have learned in my readings is the delusions that sexual predators have. Henry was no different. He truly believed that he was having a relationship with me. He knew it was wrong, but to him, I was his property. To this point, the abuse had been very much that he would have me 'wank him off', but because of his idea that we were in a relationship, he wanted to return the favour. He would use his fingers and I would sit/lie there feeling nothing but disgust. Henry frequently got really angry with me because I wasn't showing any response; *'Don't you like it this way?'* and *'Don't I turn you on?'* were questions he would ask me. In fear of his fists, I would tell him I did but just wasn't in the mood. I soon learned that I would have to do something so that these sessions could be shorter. In effect, I became an accomplished faker.

#

Ever the delusional deviant, Henry told me several times that he was not doing anything *illegal*. He had not had sex with me because I was underage and that he couldn't wait until I was sixteen so that we could do it. I can't remember how it came about, but he wanted to know if there had ever been anyone else he didn't know about and I stupidly told him about my grandad. Both me and my mum would pay for that mistake. As my sixteenth birthday came closer, I became more and more stressed, but I hid it well. I didn't know what to do, but I did know that I would not do what he wanted – he wanted me to get pregnant by him, pass it off as some boy at school, and he and mum would adopt it. Together with the events of October that year (next chapter) I was determined. Luckily for me, my doctor was quite a wise old bloke.

#

Over the time I'd been in Gateshead, I had seen my doctor quite frequently because of my very heavy periods and the pain which accompanied them. In the December before my sixteenth birthday, I went to him and told him I just couldn't cope anymore and that I'd heard going on the pill was a way to control heavy and painful periods. I was in his room for quite a while but managed to persuade him that as I was only one month off from my sixteenth birthday, my parents didn't need to know. And just like that, at 15 years and 11 months, I was on the contraceptive pill! I breathed a massive sigh of relief that afternoon – I was in control of at least one aspect of my life. What was even better, was that I was able to hold two fingers up at Henry (not literally) as he would not be able to do what he was planning.

#

There were many occasions during the presence of Henry in our lives when my mum caused me hurt. I do remember the hurt, but I am not altogether sure if I remember exactly what she said that did this. So, I'm not going to quote, just explain my take, and forgive me Mum if you read this and I've got it wrong, but I can only record it as I remember it. Indeed, this is my truth which mightn't be yours.

#

I remember one day in the summer of 1984, Mum was in their room cleaning it and I had to pop in to speak to her about something. Somehow, she had found out I was on the pill. She was mad that I had gone behind her back, although more likely disappointed in me. She called me some names in her anger and the feeling that I had let her down really hurt, but in the same sense, I was also protecting myself so the confusion just built. When I think back to this time of my life, and this moment in particular, all I feel is nothingness. A total lack of anything. I remember around the same time that Mum and I had a conversation about using tampons. Her response was basically that I would not be able to use them until I'd had sex – little did she know.

Revelation

#

I went on the pill in December of 1983 and in October (I think) of the same year, Mum had a hysterectomy. She was in hospital for a while as she'd had to have a blood transfusion and had reacted badly to it. It was at this time that I was in a relationship with Dan. One night, Dan and I had visited Mum and we were standing and waiting for the bus to take us home. As teenagers do, we were kissing and Dan went so far as to nibble my left ear – oh my god – I will never forget that feeling – the first time ever I had had a real sexual feeling. The first time I was to know what it truly felt like to have butterflies in your stomach when being touched by someone. A feeling I would not have again for many years.

#

The day after visiting Mum in hospital, I got home from school to find a very livid Henry and no Rob at home. Henry immediately set about telling me what had happened and what I was to do about it. Again, the following is just a precis of the conversation, I can't remember the exact words:

Henry: Your bastard brother's got a broken nose.
Me: How?
Henry: I gave it to him because he's only gone and told your mum that I'm abusing you.
Me: *Silence*
Henry: Well! Come on bitch – how are you going to sort this?
Me: *Silence*
Henry: I know how. I'm going to see her later and she'll accuse me. I'll tell her it's all lies and you – you'll tell her the same.
Me: *Silence* (*oh god, Mum's going to hate me*)
Henry: You know if you tell her the truth, she'll not believe you – it's all your fault anyway.

While I can't remember the exact words, the above is pretty close. My mind was in a whirl and all I could think of was what my mum would think of me. Not, as you might imagine, great, I can get away from here now. No – it was all about my mum and not letting her down. I also remember thinking about Rob – how could I do this to him? He'd stood up, he'd noticed something and been my protector and I was going to call him a liar – I knew that was what I had to do. Now as an adult, I am disgusted with myself. This was a perfect opportunity, but my mind was everywhere. What happened next sealed my fate, and before I relate this to you, I don't want anyone to blame my mother. Blame Henry and the circumstances he manipulated for all of my family.

#

The very next day, against the doctor's wishes, Mum discharged herself from the hospital.

She walked a great deal of the way back to Gateshead – she must have been in great pain.

When she got back, she asked me for the truth. I remember this as if it was 10 minutes ago. I hung my head, looked at the floor and wished I could die as the words, 'No, it's not true,' left my mouth.

#

The next thing I remember is travelling silently with Mum to Newcastle where Rob was now living with Alison (his girlfriend). Mum was going to ask him why he had made it all up. Then stopping just outside Alison's front door, Mum asked the following:
'Anna, I need to know before I go in, have you been mucking about with my man?'

In utter and total disbelief at the way she had phrased this, I replied with 'No.' I mean technically that was true because it was him 'mucking' about with me. But it was her next words which were to hurt the most, and to this day still do:

'Good, I'm glad because I don't know what I would do if you were.'

#

Now, again, the above words are not exact but are pretty damn close. Most people will have read this and thought, 'Why did she not just say yes, he has been abusing me'? And if I'm totally honest, I don't know. All I do know was the terror that was in me – terror that I can feel at this moment while recalling this time – terror that every abused child feels when faced with such a dilemma – I just wasn't strong enough.

#

Others will ask after reading my mother's words, why do I not hate her? I can't – Mum was as much a victim as me. Henry had her terrified of her own shadow by this point and she had no idea how to get out of it. It is very easy for those on the outside to say, 'Just walk away,' or 'Even a whiff of any man doing that to my kid I'd be off,' but until they have walked in the shoes of an abused child/woman/man, those people can't even begin to understand.

#

Somehow, I don't know how the situation was resolved and now Henry had exactly what he'd wanted all along – my brothers gone with no one to protect me or Mum.

#

I remember the next time I saw Dan, he held me and asked what was wrong. I told him, 'Some stuff at home'. Oh, if only it was just 'some stuff'. Dan was so caring, the way he held me and let me cry. Things really began to ramp up at home – worst was Henry going on and on (only in Mum's absence) about boys, and Dan in particular. This period is a little black to me, but I do remember being terrified of what Henry would do to Dan if I continued to see him. So, I ended my relationship with him. He was beside himself when I told him – I couldn't tell him why. It broke my heart to see his face.

When I look back to Gateshead, this is the worst time. Not because of the revelation and its repercussions, but because I broke that boy's heart. His stony silence and the way he looked at me whenever I saw him around school have stayed with me. Dan never spoke to me again! Even today this memory hurts.

It Happened

#

Sex – Henry was so excited. He couldn't wait to 'consummate' our 'relationship'.

His preparation was exact. Basically, a towel on the bed to ensure there was no blood on the sheets because of course, every virgin bleeds the first time. But I didn't!

#

I'll never forget that day, the day I had physical 'sex' for the first time. I frequently tell myself that it was the first time I had sex because I wanted to – that was my first time, but I can't accept it. Of all the things that man robbed from me, that is the one that I can't get over. Everyone has a story they can share, how they 'wished it hadn't just been a fumble in the dark,' or 'although it was painful it was so romantic' – anything other than, 'my bastard stepfather pushed me onto a towel on the bed and stuck his penis into me without any care at all!' I just lay there, inert. He kept thrusting until he made a noise and it was done.

Afterwards, he wanted to know why I had not enjoyed it, why I hadn't moved with him. All I could say was that I didn't know what to do. Worst mistake ever … he then said, in that case, it was his job to make sure I learned.

#

Then he spotted the lack of 'evidence'. His face went purple with anger, a face I had become accustomed to and was going to be seeing a lot more of over the following three years. He called me all sorts of names, wanted to know who I'd slept with before him, why wasn't he my first, etc, etc, etc. He wouldn't believe I'd not slept with anyone else. I'd had boyfriends but apart from Malcolm and Dan, they never lasted long. The violence didn't start that day, but it wasn't long in coming.

#

I will never know when I medically lost my virginity (Henry certainly took my virginity in the real sense of the word). Somewhere inside, I believe my grandfather physically took it with his fingers, but I just don't know. All these things that should be precious to a woman have been taken from me by my guardians and if I'm going to ever achieve self-acceptance, I have to find a way around this.

#

What I don't want this narrative to be about is the amount of times Henry raped me – because that is what it was – rape. Instead, I want to recount the moments I remember, and how they impacted me and those around me. Hopefully, through the writing of this narrative, I will get to the point where I can find the real me.

#

Yesterday, my son Rhys came to see me and give me a birthday gift – *The Dictionary of Obscure Sorrows by John Koenig.* I thoroughly recommend this to anyone who just wants to sit down and think about life. Essentially, the book is a collection of words created to give a name to obscure feelings that we as human beings have. Rhys said his favourite word in the book was on page 69 – 'Anoscetia' – which is defined as 'the anxiety of not knowing the real you'. How apt that I should be working on my narrative today and be thinking of the book just as I started.

#

Essentially, Koenig puts forward the idea that we see everyone around us in vibrant colour while we ourselves do not seem to be **'tinted with any particular vibe'.** He has a point as we are not aware of all that makes others them. However, my search in this narrative is really to discover if the real me is who I am. Confusing, yes – you should be in my mind. Oh wait, this whole narrative is a stream of consciousness, so you are in my mind. I hope you find it worthwhile.

#

As I said, I am not going to document the rapes because being made to have sex with Henry was at the very least, a weekly thing. And whenever Mum was away (thankfully not often) I was made to share his bed all night too. There were two occasions when I refused to have sex and both ended in violence.

#

Both events took place in The Lord Palmerston pub in Hounslow, London (more on how we got there later). The first time, Mum was serving downstairs in the pub and there were no other staff on, so Henry was content that it was fairly 'safe'. I was sitting on the sofa when he came into the lounge and told me to follow him to the bedroom. I point blank (I will cover this reference later in The Boss) looked him in the face and said 'No!' He was incredulous – how dare I say no to him. Well, I dared, and I did it again – knowing full well I would have to face the consequences of my choice. He grabbed me by the hair, pulled me onto the floor and sat on top of me – he was bloody heavy.

#

Again and again, he said he was going to fuck me and again and again I refused – I was so far into my need to stand up for myself that I would not back down. It was then that he put his hands around my throat and started choking me. He kept saying over and over again, 'You will do what I fucking tell you, when I tell you.'

I don't know how long this went on, but the next thing I remember was my mum shouting at him to get off of me. She had to push him and punch him to get through to him. By this time, my lips were blue through lack of oxygen and I had begun to lose consciousness. Thank god Mum came upstairs when she did. Do I regret making the decision to stand up for myself? NEVER! I know I could have died, but I felt so strong for having said no and for avoiding the sex on that occasion that I can never regret it.

#

As a consequence of this event, I had quite severe bruising around my neck, bruising that plainly was the result of being strangled. I had to agree to wear clothes that covered this until it was gone – I only did it for Mum. We had a cover story for when people did see it, that I had been attacked on the tube on my way home from work in the centre of London. Obviously, no one believed this, but equally, no one asked twice nor did anything about their suspicions.

#

Thinking about this episode, I believe the only reason Henry didn't force me was because he wanted to continue his bizarre belief that it was consensual. He clearly got the message because a week later when I said no again, he did force me. Violent rape is not entirely different to 'abuse' rape. Your body is still being violated, and your very sense of relevance in the world is diminished; the difference is the physical pain, the cuts and bruises, trying to walk afterwards without showing the pain in case someone asks you and you break down in tears with the humiliation of it all. I knew that day that I would not say no again. I also knew that I was getting out!

Louise and Others

#

In my readings regarding abusers, one thing that is prominent is their inability to control their urges. In fact, they need to satisfy them frequently, quite often with multiple victims – Henry was no exception. There are many, I believe, he attempted to abuse and I will not go into any great detail. However, there were a significant few where his attentions had a direct impact on me.

When we lived in Newcastle, Henry's middle daughter decided to live with us.

Following his split from their mother, they had moved to Germany and Louise was not having a good time out there. I think she probably came to regret coming to stay with us. She certainly didn't stay for long.

#

Louise and I didn't get on, well not at first. She obviously saw me as a replacement for her in her father's eyes. This changed though. Louise changed. When she arrived, she was quite present, what I mean by that is that you knew she was there. She made sure her voice was heard and made every attempt possible to be seen before me – I was more than happy for that to be the case. She probably thought I was a pushover. What she doesn't know is that I was just glad to be out of 'sight' for a short while.

#

A short time after her arrival, Louise began wetting the bed and started smoking (at least there we had something in common). She also became quieter, and less vociferous – clear signs of an abused child. Now, it could be that she changed due to the arguments, but I don't believe so. I believe that Henry had turned his attention, at times, to his own daughter. There were lots of little signs – stepping away from her when I entered the room, and her hurried altering of her clothes, to name a few. I obviously can't say for certain that he was abusing her, though I would not hesitate to bet on it.

#

Henry's eldest daughter, Amy, would never speak to him. She declared she hated him. Most people probably put that down to him leaving their mother for mine, but I feel there is more to it than that. Why? Because at the time of their split, Amy was not much older than I was when Henry started abusing me, and I don't think Henry made any exceptions regarding his victims. Years later, when Amy died suddenly due to a brain haemorrhage, Henry didn't even go to his own daughter's funeral … that really says it all!

#

Anyway, Louise left following 6 short months with us, and I remember sitting on a bus with my friend Susie not long after she had gone back. We were talking about Louise and how despite her initially getting on my nerves, that I kind of missed her. That was when Susie dropped the bombshell. Susie told me she believed she knew why; she had stayed with me a couple of weeks before this and told me on the bus that she never would again. Apparently, Henry had tried to get into bed with her that night (we were both in the same room, different beds). She told him to go away. He said he'd got the wrong room. No fucking way did he get the wrong room, and yes, I will swear because as I write this, it brings back the anger I felt at the time. Along with that anger, I felt (and still do) absolutely helpless, bereft and ashamed.

#

That day, we were going to Susie's and I remember her parents speaking to me. They didn't ask me outright – they just said they felt that my home life was not what it should be and that I could stay with them any time I wanted. They also asked, in a very pointed way, if I wanted them to help me. I was dumbstruck. We were still in Gateshead at this time, not long after Henry first raped me. Apart from Rob, no one had ever offered me help. No one had ever seemed to see me. What did I do? I said to them that I'd like nothing more, but that I didn't want my mum to get into trouble so could they please just leave it alone. They agreed unhappily. If it were today though, I don't think they would even ask because today, it is not such a taboo. I also know that if the police had ever asked me, I could never have lied to them. That would have been wrong.

#

My friendship with Susie didn't last long after that – we dwindled apart unsurprisingly. Another friend I had when we lived in Gateshead was Jill. She, like me, was a smoker (something my Grandad had introduced me to when I was just 7 years old). Henry caught me and Jill smoking in my room above the pub – he never told my mum – just another thing to hold over me.

#

Anyway, I don't know how it came about, but Henry, Jill and I went up to Scotland for a weekend. Jill and I were staying with my Aunt Pippa, so I felt safe taking Jill along – certainly safer than if I'd gone with him on my own. On the drive up we all smoked – Henry just kept supplying them. He also filled us full of sweets and chocolates and I was really sick. I can't remember anything from that trip other than that when we were at Pippa's, Jill and I sat and listened to music and smoked. What I do remember is that after we got back, Jill never spoke to me again. In fact, she completely shunned me at school and I am left wondering if Jill was just another of Henry's targets.

#

There are others I have heard of since, but theirs is not my story to tell.

The Boss

#

5th June 1985, St James Park, Newcastle. I was to encounter my celebrity love which still lasts to this day – I was 17 then, (I'm a good deal older now, and Bruce Springsteen's music still soothes my soul).

#

Mum and Henry had moved to London by this time and I was staying with a friend of Mum's in Gateshead while I finished college. Rosemary and Pippa (my aunts) had tickets to the concert, but Pippa couldn't go, so Mum bought her ticket for me. I had never heard of Springsteen, nor even heard any of his music before that day. I just went to the concert because I'd never been to one before and I wanted to do something normal teenagers did.

#

The wait outside the stadium was long and tedious (something I have repeated several times since, but definitely not a tedious wait on subsequent occasions, more one with butterflies in my stomach in anticipation of a great experience). When we finally got in, Rosemary and I ran to the front of the pitch – apparently that is what you did. I cannot recall being enamoured with his music that day, in fact, I recall being bored for part of the time. I did like the feeling of being there and I enjoyed the sound. So, as soon as I could afterwards, I listened to his music. I fell in love!

#

As the Boss was coming on stage, the cheers were deafening, but then I heard boos. Rosemary told me this was because his (then) wife, Julianne Phillips, could be seen at the side of the stage. I never did get that, I mean okay, there are those who 'fall in love' with their celebrity crush, but we do know that it is just a fantasy. Another word from Koenig's book which quite aptly deals with this is 'sonder', which essentially means that we are but a bit part in the lives of others, while our lives are complete and they are a bit part in ours. However, in the case of Springsteen being a bit part in my life, I would have to disagree.

#

So, I haven't physically met him, nor will I ever, and I am not even a bit part in his life, merely a speck of dust, but the part that Springsteen has played and continues to play in my life is more than just a 'bit.' His music is full of characters. He talks of them as all being a part of himself, how when he starts writing, he gets into their heads and that is where the music comes from. It is this that gives his songs soul. I can feel every emotion of these personas at the centre of my being. In turn, I can listen to his music and become that character. I made reference earlier to some lyrics from 'Point Blank' from Springsteen's 'River Album,' the chorus:

#

Point Blank
*****Like little white lies, you tell to ease the pain*****
*****You're walking in the sights, girl*****
*****Of point blank*****
*****And it's one false move*****
*****And baby, the lights go out*****

#

The River is an album I listened to over and over during my brief return to Scotland following this concert. My recall of this short period in Scotland during 1985 is one of my strongest, yet weakest, in that I know it happened and that it was powerful, but I don't know if I remember it exactly. Anyway, what follows is the best I can do:

#

I remember sitting in the living room of Rosemary's house. Her sister-in-law and I were babysitting Raymond who was asleep and we had the record on. The sofa was red (I think velvet) with tassels across the bottom. I was moving my fingers through the pile of the carpet, my eyes closed, completely lost in the song, especially the phrasing and notes of the words 'point blank' and how the music has a rhythm that hits you in the way a bullet might hit a body. The sensation I had directly after the words quoted above served as a wake-up call to my inner being.

#

That was the moment that I knew I had to stop being such a weakling, that my life had me in its sights and that if I wasn't careful, my lights would go out. Not literally, but figuratively.

Now I know that Springsteen's songs are full of ideas and stories that he moulded to express his own thoughts, feelings, and opinions. But with all good art, the artist leaves their work open to interpretation and to be 'used' by the audience in a manner befitting them. I did this and still do this with Springsteen's work (and others of all genres of art) and I will forever be thankful for being introduced to the work of Springsteen; music which speaks to my soul, music which has been with me through the good times and has given me a platform through which to breathe during the not so good times. I have to say, I'd love to sit down with Bruce and discuss the impact his music has had on me and thank him ... but then, so would millions of others!

#

The other advantage is that Springsteen's work sounds even better loud, and was very annoying to Henry – I wonder, was he jealous that I looked to another the way I looked to the Boss?

A Few Months in Scotland

#

I got your hopes up there, didn't I? You thought that from here on in, I was going to describe how I stopped being such a weakling and stood up for myself – wrong on so many levels!

First and foremost, all that I am going to relate to you now, I did not understand at the time what I was doing. It is only now as an adult, one who has gone through counselling three times, that I am able to verbalise a possible motive for my behaviour during these months.

Mum and Henry had moved to London, and the brewery didn't want them to have me there until their 6-month probation was up, so I returned to Scotland after my college course had finished. This was a very turbulent time for me. I was free from Henry, but I was adrift; I had no purpose in life. I was surrounded by my family, yet felt as if I didn't belong with them or anywhere. I did not know who I was. I had a job for a little while – in a sheep fleece sorting factory. Oh my god, it was stinking! I didn't last long. Apart from that, I was on the dole – £17 a week – I had to pay £12 a week rent to my aunt.

I wish I could remember this time more clearly – my mum knows more about it than I do. She knows because people enjoyed telling her just how much of a slut I was. My memories of that time are merely feelings. I know I slept with a lot of men ... you would have thought I would want to get away from that, but in reality, it was the only thing I knew how to do. I know I hurt some of them. I even got engaged at one point – I can't even remember his name. All I do remember is that he was tall and had a very small penis. My motive, I believe, was to control men rather than have them control me. A way to get back at the male species who had done nothing but wrong to me. It is very sad, really, that my actions were looked down upon and talked about, that I was treated like dirt by many, and yet they all knew about Henry. What did they do – nothing!

The best way to describe this time is to give you a typical Friday/Saturday night. I would drink a little while getting ready to go out. I often went out with my older brother Rob or with Rosemary (others too, but I can't remember). We would frequently end up in Jackie 'O's nightclub, usually during happy hour so that we could get as much alcohol as possible for our money. Once I'd had a few drinks, men would be just queuing up to buy me more (now I know it wasn't because of my looks, but my reputation). I would always leave with a strange man. We'd end up having a quick fumble in some doorway or alcove and he'd stick me in a taxi (which he paid for) to take me home. I remember no faces, no names, nothing. I feel nothing but deep sadness about that time of my life. I wanted to be in control, but in reality, I was still being controlled.

One day though, Charlie (Rosemary's husband) asked me why I did it. He asked me if Henry had been abusing me. I was shocked. I didn't know they suspected, but Rob had obviously told them. I clearly remember this moment – it's as if it is happening again right now. I had a flash in my head of a gun going off and decided I had to speak up. I told him that Rob was right. It felt good to say it out loud at last. Charlie was great. He told me I was better than that, and that I could do anything I wanted. I didn't need to have sex with anyone and everyone. I was a good person. I'm sitting here crying as I write this – this is the first time I've been able to actually cry in a long time and it feels good.

I think I might be crying for my lost childhood, or for the fact that someone cared enough to reach out to me at that very, very low point of my life. Charlie and Rosemary told me they were going to let my mum know. In the end, it was Evelyn who told my mum.

Later that day, Mum called me. She was beside herself and swore she had no idea. She said she would leave him, move back to Scotland and we could get a council house together and start over. Oh – I had one whole day thinking that my life was about to get so much better; I was wrong.

The next day, Mum called again. Henry had persuaded her to stay (I was later to realise that this must have been achieved through the use of his fists). I stayed in Scotland.

I did have some happy moments during that stay in Scotland – his name, Ron Whyte. I first knew Ron when we were just 5 years old. He, Simon Burns and I were good friends at primary school. We all lived close together (I was Simon's girlfriend at primary). Ron and I got together during my time in Scotland that year and I stayed faithful to him. There were two reasons for this. Firstly, I connected with him. He wasn't some random stranger and he genuinely cared for me. Also, after Charlie's 'pep' talk, I wasn't prepared to be just a 'bike' anymore.

Ron's mum did not like me. She'd obviously heard about my reputation and warned me off. She actually used the words, 'I know your type, and you're not good enough for my son'. She was wrong though. Ron fell in love with me and I had some very strong feelings for him. It was probably love, but for many, many years, I was numb and unable to really love. I was Ron's first, and that is a very, very special thing for me. I know that if I had stayed in Scotland, Ron and I would have lasted. But I didn't and he went on to marry a beautiful woman on the very same day that I married my first husband. The difference, he's still married to her. I'm not married to Brian anymore.

Return to Hell

#

This is the part of my narrative that many will find difficult to reconcile with. In truth, I still find it difficult at times. However, I am not ashamed of my decision – it was the right thing for me at that moment in my life.

#

During my time in Scotland, I lived with Rosemary, then Evelyn, and to be honest, they got fed up with me. I wasn't earning money, I showed no signs of being able to fully support myself and they had families of their own to care for. I felt unwanted, unwelcome and quite frankly, a burden. Despite having a strong relationship with Ron, I was in a fit of despair and wanted nothing more than to be with my mum. I know, you are all going to be thinking, why? Well, I love my mum. Despite everything, we have a bond that can't be broken. Some might say that everything we endured together creates a specific glue for our bond. So, when Mum phoned just before Christmas to ask if I wanted to move down to London, I considered it and eventually decided to go.

I didn't make the decision lightly. I weighed up all my options. If I stayed in Scotland, I couldn't see the prospect of a career for myself. I knew that in London, I would have a lot more opportunities to put my secretarial training to use. That, and being with my mum were the deciding factors. Henry had promised Mum he would not 'abuse' me again. I knew that was a lie, but I was willing to take the risk. I also thought that I was, by now, strong enough to keep him at arm's length.

#

Hell is a part of the title of this chapter, and hell is what the first 18 months in London were for me. When I got there, I remember standing in the private kitchen of the pub, (The Queen's Head) when Henry came in. His first words were, 'You know I'm not going to leave you alone, don't you?' I thought then, 'What have you done Jane, why didn't you just stick it out up in Scotland?'

His face that night was smug, his intention was clear – to make my life hell and take as much pleasure from it and my body as he wanted. I also knew I'd fight, but that it would be futile.

#

There were no curtains for the window of my room in that pub, so Mum had put a very thick blanket at the window, therefore, when I went to bed, the darkness was total. I remember lying in bed and 'feeling' the door open. Assuming it was Henry, I told him to go away, I then felt the door close and breathed a sigh of relief only to have it dispelled seconds later as I felt a weight on the end of the bed. I curled into a ball and told him to just go away, I didn't want him anywhere near me. At that, the weight lifted and mere seconds later, there was a blue light in the corner of my room. The light formed the outline of someone sitting in the chair in that corner and I felt peace. No one spoke, but I knew the spirit who visited me that night (and has done since) was my great-grandmother. My nan had delivered me during a stormy night, and while she died when I was just two years old, I have always felt her with me.

#

My nan has visited me often. At a spiritualist meeting when I was in Scotland that year, I had a message to thank me for cleaning her house. I have to say I was nonplussed at this – I had been cleaning Evelyn's house that day as she was hoping for a 'swap' with another council tenant but had absolutely no understanding as to why I would get that message. Later, I found out that my nan was the first person to live in that house when it was built. I had always believed in the spirit world – that was the day any misgivings I might have had vanished. The visit from my nan that night made me realise that no matter what, I would survive whatever was to come.

#

The time that we stayed in The Queen's Head saw the rise and frequency of Henry's brutality. He stopped asking me to join him and just told me where to be and when. I tried to avoid it, but the repercussions were just so much worse that it wasn't worth it. The worst was when Mum went up to Scotland for a few days and I had my period – Henry made me sleep in his bed. I had to lie on a towel. He didn't have sex with my body (because that is how I saw it). He just wanted me there, as if we did have a relationship! I will never, ever forget the teasmaid. Having to make sure that I set it up at night so that we could sit and have a cup of tea together in bed in the morning. My husband, Peter, would like us to have one – that will never happen. Never!

#

Henry's abuse of Mum and I was always worse when he was drinking. Quite often, after all the punters were gone, he would have one of us cook him deep-fried sausage and chips. Mum and I couldn't go upstairs for fear of upsetting him, so we would stay in the bar while he continued to down pints and whisky. He would become quite maudlin sometimes and I remember him once being quite angry that he'd had a dream that when I got married, he didn't get to give me away. Inside my head, I knew I would rather never get married than have him walk me down the aisle, but I also knew that if I said that to him, he'd get violent. So, I spent at least two hours that night putting his mind at rest.

#

Reading this, you are probably thinking, 'That doesn't sound too bad'. But when you have been working almost non-stop since 8 a.m. and it is now 2 a.m. and all you want to do is get to sleep, that is abuse. Henry really ramped up the mental cruelty while we were in that pub. It only got worse when we moved to The Lord Palmerston in Hounslow.

#

Hounslow

\#

The Lord Palmerston. Named after a politician, so it seems fitting then that this is where I really began my fight for freedom, even though I had no idea what I was doing.

\#

Many things happened in the time we lived here:

\#

- My great Uncle Sam, his wife and two children came to stay.
- I deliberately dated men that I knew Henry would have an apoplexy if he knew – Asian, Irish, soldiers, criminals and worst of all customers.
- Henry violently raped me.
- Henry's physical violence towards us got much worse.
- I went to social services for help – they refused.

\#

So, let's deal with this – I wanted to hit back at Henry, I wanted him to know that he couldn't control me, and that is why I deliberately dated men that he would despise me being with. He never found out! In reality, therefore, did I hit back? Many will say no, but to me at the time, I was winning. He couldn't stop me from seeing them, and I was able to do what I wanted. Luckily for me, by this time, he'd stopped stalking me! However, I wasn't the complete slut that I had been in Scotland. I didn't sleep with any of them. I did use them though. I used them to make me feel stronger. By being able to say no to them, I was able to say no to Henry. The difference being, they accepted and respected my right to say no.

#

I don't know how long Sam and his family were with us, but I do know that they stayed in the flat below us and heard every beating my mother and I took. One that stays particularly vivid in my mind is the night I woke to hear a terrible banging noise. It sounded like a sledgehammer pummelling wood. It was, in fact, my mother's head. Mum was sitting on a seat of the three-piece suite and Henry was punching her so hard that her head meeting the wood inside the sofa chair was making that noise. I could hear Sam and Elaine below arguing, making out words that suggested he wanted to intervene but Elaine wouldn't let him. I wanted to call the police, but we didn't have mobiles then and I was too petrified to move.

Henry must have heard everyone because he stormed out of the lounge and into their room, where we heard him snoring very loudly shortly after.

#

I heard my mum then, softly crying. Not loud sobs, nothing like that, just a soft murmur. Sam and Elaine went quiet and I assume they just went back to bed. They moved out not long after. I can't remember what I did then – my mind is a complete blank. I want to think that I went through to Mum and held her, helped her in some way, but in my heart, I know that she would not have wanted that, so I can only think that I went back to sleep. Mother's face was a riot of colours for days. I felt utterly and totally ashamed of myself every time I saw her bruises. Why? Because usually, Mum took beatings when I had refused to have sex with Henry, or when he could tell for definite that I faked it. So, it was my fault – I had lit the fuse which led to his explosive violence towards my mother.

#

Below is a picture from a 'free drawing' session with Jenny. I drew all these individual objects realising as I did, they made me think of a circus, apart from the knife that is. This is why we named it the performer.

#

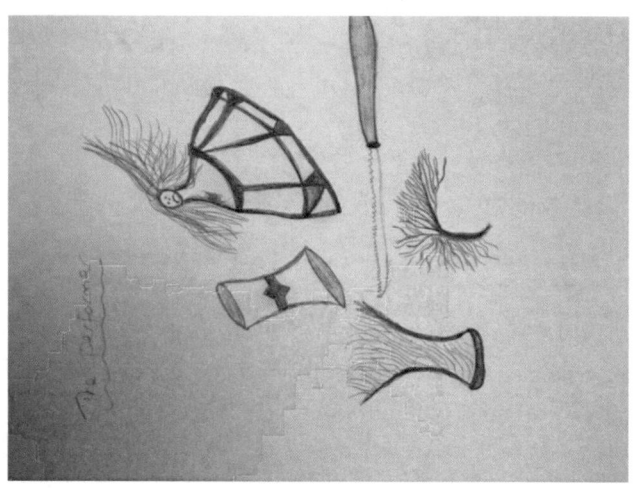

#

I suppose you could say I had to perform to survive, but in reality, Henry was the performer. One of his most memorable performances involved the knife in the drawing. I have already told you of the time Mum stopped Henry from killing me – the knife performance is when we stupidly stopped him from killing himself. Actually, the coward wouldn't have done it. He was merely being melodramatic in order to manipulate us. Henry was very irrational and quite often his rages would appear out of nowhere and have no rhyme nor reason. This was one of those cases. He was accusing me and Mum of not loving him (well – yeah!) and was holding a knife to his wrists, threatening to kill himself. He also threatened us. I remember it now as clearly as if he is right in front of me.

#

His brown nylon trousers were stained from where he couldn't be bothered to dry himself, and his top was of a dark colour of which I am not entirely sure, but I think it was a rugby top.

However, it is his face that remains solid. His hair was in the style of Elvis, and his face was fat and rectangular in shape. He was on his knees in front of me, screwing his eyes up and holding the bread knife (yes, a bread knife) horizontally to his wrist. I remember looking at it and thinking, 'Please do it – make sure you take your time and saw away', while at the same time telling him he was wrong. That we did care for him – total bollocks of course – but he would never go through with it and I just wanted to go to bed. This type of ending to our days was frequent, and quite frankly, I got bored of having to be constantly alert to what he was saying so that I didn't say the wrong thing. Even though he was a coward, I always believed that he was capable of sticking a knife into me in a fit of rage.

#

So, when I said 'fighting back' earlier, I didn't mean anything major. It was just saying no and doing things he would hate to wind him up.

#

I also said earlier that I would not detail the rapes as they were too great in number, but the one I feel I need to excise happened at the Lord Palmerston. I have no recollection of why it happened other than that I said no, and I can only assume I refused when he was in a particularly bad mood. I do know he'd been drinking, although not enough that he was incapable. It took place in our lounge and Mum was downstairs in the bar with no one to relieve her. This was not always a guarantee that she'd not come upstairs but he didn't care. Sometimes, I think he wanted her to walk in and think I was having an affair with him.

#

Anyway, the sofa was pink and he pushed me off onto the floor. He put his hand over my mouth as I started to yell for help, (I did try on this occasion), because there was something in his eyes that told me he had every intention of hurting me. I don't want to go into any more detail but I was left badly bruised in my genital area, with lots of cuts and scratches where he used his belt. My wrists were also bruised.

#

I decided to do something about it – I went to social services for help. I remember sitting in this cold, bland room and I told the woman everything, from the day Henry walked into our lives, to the night before when he had violently raped me. Her response was one of pity. I did not want her pity, I wanted her help. And here is what was wrong with society at that time (and I believe to a small part now) – I was asked what I wanted. My response was that I wanted to get out and to have somewhere safe to be. She told me I could have that, but only if I pressed charges against him. Even though I told her that I couldn't because of what it would do to Mum, she refused to help me.

#

I had never, in my life, nor have I ever since, felt so alone.

Escape

#

I knew that moving to London was the way forward for me professionally, and I was right. I joined a temp agency as soon as I moved there and I was posted to Trusthouse Forte as an office junior. By the end of the first week, I was asked to become a permanent member of staff.

#

I loved my job. I worked hard and was a stickler for getting it right. Principally, I spent my days entering data using the numeric keypad of my computer, but I also made sure that I shadowed the work of the secretaries, observing how they behaved and so forth. This paid off as after just a few months, the Group Finance Manager's secretary left and he asked if I would like the job – I never had to interview. After my first day as his secretary, he told me that his boss (The Group Financial Controller) had commented on how much of a worker I was and that he'd been wrong to doubt my abilities.

#

It was while I was at THF that I met Brian. The kindest man you will ever meet. Our first kiss happened to be on 14th February 1987 in the Cafe Royal at the end of the annual dinner and dance. I wore a knee-length white flapper dress. I had gone to the dance with a friend but spent the majority of the evening with Brian. The buttons of his suit jacket kept getting caught on the loops of my dress, frequently. I knew that night that he was special, but I was also afraid of getting too close.

Anyway, at the end of the night, Brian kissed me – I went home happy. My friend and I left the Cafe Royal and got the tube back to Hounslow. I was on a high – nothing could bring me down – or so I thought. We arrived back at the pub and were just about to open the door when my mum barged out, slammed the door shut, locked it, put the keys back through the letter box and told us to run.

#

We did, only stopping a couple of minutes later when Mum asked us to. It was then that I saw her face. She had a broken nose, her eyes were the deepest black I'd ever seen, (she could hardly see out of one of them) and I think she also had some broken ribs. It turns out that during the evening, a man had asked Henry where I was. This man was a soldier. I'd seen him around the pub and spoken to him a few times, but that was it. Henry had been in the army and was adamant that I would never date a soldier. He knew what they were like, apparently. He obviously believed that all men were utter and total deviants like himself. Anyway, Henry took the soldier's simple inquiry as to whether I was working or not and blew it all the way up to me and this soldier being in a relationship. Unfortunately, not true. He was rather good-looking and fit.

#

As was always the case with him, the possible narrative of my connection to the soldier escalated from there and Henry just lost it. My mother paid the price and she didn't want me to do so too. We walked the streets of London that night, not knowing what to do. At one point, a police car was passing slowly – I mean there we were, two 19-year-olds in their glad rags with my mother looking like she'd gone 10 rounds with Tyson and lost. Of course they were going to stop and ask if we needed help – no! I had to flag them down. They looked at Mum, and asked what happened and if she was going to press charges. When she said no, they just wound the window up and drove off! Even now, I question why I didn't just give up there and then. That was twice I'd asked for help from official sources and twice shunned.

#

Long story short, I spent the last of my wages from that month on a stinking B&B so we could get a very few hours of sleep. The next day, we returned to the pub (I hoped to find him hanging from a rope – no such luck). I never saw my friend after that day.

#

My relationship with Brian grew and I didn't want Henry to stop it like he had every other. I knew I had to do something, but I didn't know what. That something came in the form of my saviour – my mum's Uncle Sam.

#

One day, as I got off the tube in Hounslow on the way back from work, who was there but Sam. He asked me to go for a drink with him – there was a pub right there – so I did. To this day, I will never know if he was there intentionally, but as soon as we sat down, he asked me about the time I had the marks on my neck and that he didn't buy the 'bullshit' Mum and I had spun. So, I told him it all. The violence didn't come as a surprise as he had witnessed it when they stayed with us, but the sexual abuse did. He had suspicions that something else was going on but he just didn't know what. Then he said the magic words – come and live with me and April (by this time he was divorced from Elaine – April is his daughter).

#

I jumped at the opportunity. As it happened, Henry was off to some brewery function the next day and would be away all day. Sam said he would pick me and all my stuff up during his lunch hour. When I got home, I had to behave as if nothing was different – that I wasn't about to be released from my private prison. It was tough. Even tougher was telling my mum (I'm sure she could have come if she wanted). I told her that night before we went to bed so that she would have no time to persuade me otherwise. I actually don't think she would have been capable of doing so.

#

The following morning, I listened as Henry left. I gave it 20 minutes to make sure he wouldn't be coming back and started throwing all my stuff into black bags and one suitcase. I remember picking up my Springsteen LPs and just holding them, telling him that we were going to a new home where I would be safe. At the back of the pub, there was a metal staircase (much like the ones you see in American films) which led from the kitchen down to the backyard where the deliveries were made. I took all my belongings down there so that I was ready for Sam. On my last trip down, I said goodbye to Mum. My heart was aching. I wanted her to come with me, but I knew she wouldn't even if I had asked. I also knew that I had to get out; I had to be safe. Her last words to me that day were, 'I can't believe you're leaving me here to deal with him alone'.

#

That was the one time, the only time that I have ever looked at my mum and felt real anger. I am glad I felt anger because if I hadn't, I probably would have taken everything back to my room and stayed. I don't think Mum will remember saying those words. I know from many conversations with her lately, that she remembers very little detail of those years and I'm glad of that. I just hope that if you read this mum, you will realise just how much of a good thing you did for me that day. I love you.

Moving On

\#

Brian lived in a little bedsit in Peckham and that is where we had sex for the first time. He had a single bed, but also a double bed settee. We used to lie there on Sunday mornings eating chocolate digestives and melon – what a combination, but we loved it. It was very early in our relationship when I told Brian about Henry and my past. I even told him about my 'slutty' days in Scotland. He cried. I looked at him and asked why, and his response was that he wished he'd been there to stop it from happening. He was there now and I knew I was safe. This man loved me for me, no other reason. But I didn't know if I loved him, not for any reason other than I didn't know what love was.

\#

Not long after this, Brian and I moved into a house which we shared with Joe – his best friend. Sam had provided me with a home for a little while which was enough to create a bridge between my past and my future. Now, I was living with the man I was to marry, in London. We would eventually move out of this house into our first 'owned' property; a flat at No 41 Burford Road, Catford.

#

After Brian proposed, we discussed the wedding (as you might expect) and he was adamant that Henry would not walk me down the aisle. I was not, in any way, going to argue with him. He suggested my granddad. Well, I hadn't told Brian about Granddad, so I wasn't ready for that. To be honest, what I had gone through at the hands of Henry had almost pushed my grandfather's abuse into insignificance. So, I kept quiet and allowed that to happen.

#

As you can imagine, this caused quite a stramash, in fact, it meant my mother and I didn't talk for a few months. Eventually, we came to a compromise that Henry was happy with. Henry would make the 'father-of-the-bride' speech.

#

Our wedding day was blissful, only marred by the physical presence of those two men, but I managed to ignore them for the most part. Thinking about 'the-father-of-the-bride speech', I have absolutely no recollection of the content. What I do remember is sitting there, staring at my hands, at my shiny wedding ring, dreaming about my future with Brian. Occasionally, I looked up, pretending to listen, but on the whole, his speech just happened. I remember Brian's speech though, how he started and then had to sit down momentarily when he realised that the wedding might have been my funeral (it's a long story, but Mum and I were in a car accident the week before). I remember looking at him and wondering if what I was feeling was really love. I felt safe, warm and cherished. I knew that this man would move heaven and earth for me – if those feelings meant that I loved him, then I did love him, very much.

If I ever thought that getting married would end the impact of Henry on my life, I was wrong. Brian and I settled into married life and I took to it like a duck to water. I was promoted at work – well basically, the big boss's secretary had left and I was doing her job temporarily. After a few weeks, I just went into Peter Clayton's office and asked why he didn't just give me the job! He said my shorthand wasn't up to it. I told him I'd fix that so he gave me the job. If only everything was as easy to sort.

#

As I said, Brian and I were happy. Our sex life was probably no different to that of most married couples. The difference was, I continually questioned whether I was good enough. I kept telling him that I didn't think I loved him, that I didn't know what love was. He told me that even if I didn't, I would grow to love him fully and that he had enough love for the two of us. There were many occasions (and even now) when I would have to take deep breaths when touched, to remind myself that the man touching me was someone I wanted to do so. I had flashbacks; apparently, I spoke in my sleep a lot. According to Brian, we had full-on conversations while I was asleep about Henry. I was content with Brian. I now know that I did love him. I always knew I wanted to have children with him.

#

We both wanted a family, and we both wanted to raise them somewhere less 'lethal' than London. We knew that to do this we would have to live somewhere where we could drive, so we set about learning. I took my time, but Brian, well, he did a one-week crash course because he had been headhunted for a job in Brecon in Powys, South Wales – he could only accept if he could drive. We both passed first time! When we moved to Wales, we had already been trying for a child for over a year.

#

Passing a test to drive a lethal weapon proved a lot easier than getting pregnant. However, after fertility treatment, our first child, Jack Neil Wilson Jones, came along on 19th November 1992. Now I knew what love was; the strength of that immediate bond almost blew me apart.

#

So here it was – motherhood, looking down at this tiny human, his dark eyes staring back. His trust in me was absolute. How could I possibly be up to this job? The enormity of the task I'd taken on was almost overwhelming. I made a promise to each of my children, which was always a special moment. For Jack, it was when we were sat in the window of our home at 3.45 a.m. on a clear night looking at the stars. Rosie was on a day when Jack was at playgroup and we were having a cuddle on the sofa. Rhys was when he'd been awake for two solid hours. I was so tired and just sat rocking him during that beautiful moment when the birds began to wake. Finally, Evan heard my promise when he was just three days old, on a cold February morning when everyone else was fast asleep upstairs. Evan and I were just chilling in the lounge. The promise I made to all of them was:

#

My darling, I will be with you every step of the way,
I will love you unconditionally,
I will teach you right from wrong,
How to be kind, how to love.
I will laugh with you
and cry with you, most of all,
I will keep you safe from harm.

#

Always know that you are loved and you are safe.

#

The above words, or some version of them, are said by most mothers – I am sure of this. I have lived by these words and have four beautiful adult children who are leading their own lives now, being their own person and I am very proud of each and every one of them.

#

During my pregnancy with Jack, my grandfather died – he was 73 and had suffered a long painful death with prostate cancer (just what I'd wished for). I remember his funeral was on quite a miserable day in September of '92. The service was held at the house before internment at the cemetery. I stood over his grave, heavily pregnant with Jack and cried as they lowered the coffin – not because he was dead, but because I'd never told anyone about what he'd done, because I wanted to have the words *you are a dirty, shitty bastard* said as he was laid to 'rest' and didn't have the courage to do so. I did, however, return to his grave a couple of years after and tell him exactly what I thought.

#

Brian did something that day that really made me smile. During the wake, Henry was holding court and Brian told him, in front of everyone, that he was nothing but a stinking bastard. My god, I don't know what surprised them the most, the fact that Brian, quiet, timid Brian, could use such language or that he had challenged Henry in that way in front of everyone. Henry, like all cowards when faced with the truth, said nothing.

#

Now my granddad's name was 'Neil' and you might think, why name your child after that man? At the time of naming him, Brian still didn't know about the abuse and he wanted us to follow tradition regarding family names – Wilson being his mother's maiden name. I personally and internally and still to this day agreed to Neil as it was also my dad's name. For me, Jack's middle name is after the man who raised me.

#

One of the very last times I can remember Henry being in my presence was at Jack's christening. He held Jack and I never took my eye off him. Every second my boy was held by that man made me feel sick. I swore to myself that day that he would never be able to have close contact with him again. I held true to my word.

The Family Grew

And so did my strength. After a second round of fertility drugs, Brian and I were pregnant with our second child. I remember clearly the day before my period was due, walking back from Abergavenny town centre to the car when I told him I was pregnant.

#

I was wearing blue leggings with flowers on – all the rage then – and a white t-shirt with one flower that matched the leggings. Jack was in his pushchair and we were crossing the road when I blurted out, 'I am pregnant, it's a girl and I want to call her Rosemary'. Brian, used to my ability to just 'know' said, 'OK, if you are right can we call her Rosie for short'. Hence our daughter was named before she was officially confirmed to exist. Jack had arrived almost 5 weeks early, but Rosie kept me waiting – she was only two weeks early. Her full name, Rosemary Pippa White Jones is in homage to my grandmother. Yes, I know you are all thinking 'How could you do that after she treated you the way she did?' The honest answer is I don't know. What I do know is that Rosie suits the name – she owns the name. It is her! Despite everything, my gran owned her life – she lived it the way she wanted – so perhaps having 'Pippa White' as the middle names was apt.

#

Rosie's birth fuelled my strength. If I was not letting Henry be close to my son, there was absolutely no way on this god-given earth that he would ever be in the same building as my daughter, let alone the same room. To this end, when Rosie was less than two weeks old, I wrote a letter to my mother. In it, I told her that I wanted Henry out of our lives, he was never to be around me, my husband or my children. I made it quite clear that I was doing this to protect my children as he was a paedophile. I calmly wrote that we would be civil to him at family gatherings and that she was welcome any time she wanted to visit and spend as much time with her grandchildren as she wished.

#

Her reply was a very strongly worded letter, essentially accusing me of not knowing what rape was … and so forth, and if that was how I felt, then so be it. She was angry, upset and for the second time in our relationship, my mother stopped talking to me. This was quite a difficult time for me. Even though I lived in Wales and Mum lived all the way up in Scotland, she was always on the end of the phone if I needed to talk, ask for advice about motherhood, etc. At that moment in my life, when I needed it most, that avenue was lost to me.

The absurdity of this situation became clear when Rosie was just 8 months old and my little brother, Frank, got married. Brian, the children and I stayed at Gran's. The whole experience was surreal. We never spoke to Mum – she never spoke to us. Ironically, there is a picture of me, Gran, Mum and Rosie – the four generations of females – a picture my mum asked someone to take. It is not a picture that tells a story as we all look 'normal'. Only those in the picture (except Rosie) can see the invisible chasm that lies between my mother and me. Worse, the pain that lies behind that picture still sits with me today.

#

While we were in Scotland for Frank's wedding, Gran had told me and Brian that we had our 'pigeon pair' and should stop now. Two was more than enough. I always wanted more children. Brian is the middle child of five and I am the middle child of three. I have never liked odd numbers, so we decided we'd have four.

#

There are moments in our lives that are etched, not just in our minds, but in our hearts and our eyes too. To date, most of those I have recounted for you have not been good. Some have and I'd like to add another to that now – July 1995. Jack was in a toddler group, and Rosie was lying face down on her play mat – a circular one with a padded edge so that she could have tummy time independently. I was sat in the armchair – a size 10-12, wearing a red tartan mini-skirt and a strappy light blue top. I was happy. Then Rosie lifted her head up, opened her eyes and gave me the biggest smile. Even now as I write this, the momentous feeling I experienced returns. My heart swells, I see her there in her cream babygro with the little red roses on and I know, I just know, that was the moment I realised she and I would have a special relationship.

#

We'd planned to essentially have two sets – Jack and Rosie with a four-year gap and then another two close together so that each 'set' if you like, had a playmate. With that in mind, we asked Dr Johnston how long we should try before having fertility treatment when we next wanted a child. He responded with, 'Try longer next time – a year. For some reason, after having a female child, sometimes it kick-starts the ovaries into working better'.

So, me being me, thought if our plan was going to work then I wanted to get pregnant when Rosie was three and a bit. That meant if we had to try for a year, then we should start when she was two. We couldn't wait and started trying before she was two – well, I must have got pregnant straight away because I found out I was pregnant, with number three, just the day before Jack's fourth birthday, which was two days after Rosie's second!

#

Rhys Robert Jones was due to arrive on 26th July 1997. When I told my best friend Lynne the news, we both said at the same time, 'You do know he will arrive on 3rd July', this being the date 6 years previously she had given birth to her daughter (my god-daughter) who had died in the womb at full term. Sure enough, 2 minutes to midnight on the 2nd, I went into labour and Rhys arrived 2 1/2 hours later on the 3rd. Lynne, as she had been with the other two, was with me – what a star. Now for the name – how did Rhys get his name? Well, with the first two, it was easy; their first names are my two favourites – Brian didn't have a say (sorry). We both decided that this little one's name had to have another reason for being, one that meant he was fearless because who chooses to come into a family where your siblings are so young? Hence, he was christened Rhys Robert.

#

We made a decision then to have the fourth so that they were close to the other three and found ourselves pregnant again in early 2000. This would have meant a 2-year gap, a 2 ½-year gap and then a 3-year gap. Unfortunately, though, we lost that little one and although very early in the pregnancy I am sure it was a girl and I have internally always thought of her as Rae. The day I miscarried was 2nd April 2000, Brian's birthday and also Mother's Day. I will never forget that day, nor will I forget my little rainbow Rae.

#

Rosie had clearly sorted my ovaries out though, because getting pregnant seemed to just happen to me now. In June of that same year, we were pregnant with our fifth and last child. Again, we wanted to have a special name for the baby and felt that as he had held on in there despite threatening to go the same way as his sister had earlier that year, he needed a name that showed his strength. Brian chose his name; we went for Evan Lloyd Jones, both names meaning strong, steadfast and true. And with that, on 16th February 2001, our family was complete.

#

When I was pregnant with both Jack and Rosie, I suffered heavy blood loss at 12 weeks. It was never confirmed, but I have always wondered and often felt that they were twins. In fact, with Jack, they were going to do a 'scrape' but I asked them to check first. Thank goodness they did because his little heart was as strong as an ox on the scan. If they were indeed twins, then their 'rainbow other halves' are looking down.

#

My children are my life: Jack, Rosie, Rhys, (Rae) and Evan – I love you!

Peter

\#

What can I say? The previous couple of chapters have presented you with an idyllic life. Marriage to a successful man who worshipped the ground I walked on, a healthy sex life (despite my past) and four beautiful, healthy children. This, some might say should be the end of the story. A happy ending with the abused child evolving into a happy adult. But life is never that simple. Thoughts and feelings are never that simple.

\#

This part of my narrative is going to be one of the hardest to write. Why? Because it is a time of my life of which I am both ashamed and elated by…

\#

By this time, Brian and I were living in our forever home – a beautiful four-bedroomed house which was on a corner plot. The garden backs onto a wooded area where we walked the dog, took the children to explore and generally had an amazing life. I was very happy there, or at least I thought I was. I am not going to hide the truth – I have promised you that from the start, so I need to say that throughout my marriage to Brian, although I was always faithful to him, I did flirt shamelessly whenever I was out. Many times I was approached by admirers. Sometimes, I accepted their advances, but until 2003, in my eyes, I was faithful. I didn't sleep with these men. I loved Brian – I still love Brian. The love I have for him though is not the sort of love that I encountered when I dropped Jack at football one Friday night before taking the others to our holiday caravan in New Quay, South Wales. Brian would pick Jack up later and join us for the weekend.

#

I remember I was wearing typical middle-class, stay-at-home Mum clothes; relaxed trousers with a loose-fitting (but expensive) blouse. The car was packed to the gunnels with everything needed for the weekend. I left the other three in the car as I walked with Jack across to the field. It was his second session – Jack had told me the coach was called Peter and I was to make sure he knew that Brian would be picking Jack up.

#

I approached one of the dads and asked who Peter was and he pointed to this tall man, though how tall I didn't know until he stood up. Peter had his left foot on a rock tying the laces of his boot. He was wearing red tracksuit bottoms and a Man

Utd. top. His hair was mid-brown, wavy and sat just below his ears – he also had the beginnings of a penalty spot on his crown. I physically stopped for a second and in my head I heard the words, 'You'll marry him'. Jack spotted him, dragged me over and that was when Peter stood up – all 6 ft 2" of him. I blurted out what I'd come to say, handed over Jack's fees and walked back to the car. I could swear I felt his eyes on me.

#

I changed at that moment. Of course, my mind was telling me not to be stupid, to put the sudden rush of feeling to the side, to ignore it and squash it. I was married and I loved my husband and my kids. To begin with, it worked. A few weeks later, Rosie and I took a trip to Scotland to celebrate Rosemary's 40th – it was a really good weekend. But I spent most of it thinking about Peter – I'd not seen him in a few weeks because I'd just drop Jack off, watch him run to the safety of the coaches and get Brian to pick him up. I swore that weekend that I would avoid seeing Peter if I could because I couldn't bear the thought of hurting Brian and the kids.

#

Fate, however, disagreed. Two days after my return, I was in the Co-op in Brecon, and there, right in front of me, was Peter. He was wearing a long wax coat and a hat (a bit like a cowboy one) – I should say at this point that Peter is a farmer (Brian is a Company Secretary – legal stuff). You could not get two more different people if you tried. Anyway, he turned to me and smiled – like a silly little schoolgirl, all I could think was that he'd remembered who I was. We passed pleasantries and I went home.

#

If when I went home, I had felt the same as before I went out to the shop that day, I would have cut all ties. I'd have told Brian and arranged for Jack to play football elsewhere or avoided the situation totally. But I didn't. There was, and still is, an ache in the middle of my chest to be with Peter. I did not make my decision lightly, even when Peter and I started talking – for that was all it was. I was still fighting internally to stay with Brian, to always be with him and the kids, to keep our family together.

#

So, how did you start talking I hear you ask? I can't remember how, or even why, but I ended up coaching the girls at the club. On the first night, Peter loaned me a whistle which I forgot to give back to him. The next day, I texted him to say I had his whistle – his reply was quite suggestive. I remember looking at it, knowing that this was the crunch point – if I replied in one way he'd get 'the' message that I was not interested. The other – well, let's just say, I took the second option. The 'talking' we embarked on that day was, to say, the least dirty. Some of the things that passed between us reminded me of my past but it didn't bother me – that really confirmed for me that what I felt for Peter was totally different to Brian. Even so, even while this was going on, I still held onto the idea that I could walk away at any moment and that my family would remain intact.

#

The moment I made my choice, the choice was made for me.

#

It was January 2004. I was at college (I was studying an Access to Higher Education Course) when Peter texted to say that his wife, Olive knew and that she had Brian's number. This very angry woman (rightly) had called Brian and left a message saying his wife was having an affair with her husband. Now, I would argue that it was not strictly true. To this point, all we had done was talk and have the occasional kiss along with snatched two-minute meetings when I was out with my friends clubbing.

#

I went straight home and waited for Brian. I was surprisingly calm. I had absolutely no idea what I was going to do. I knew I wanted to be with Peter, but I also knew I loved Brian. The moment he opened the door he asked me. I told him it was true but I had not had sex with Peter. Brian gasped and turned white. It was that look of such deep hurt and pain that made up my mind. Most will say I should have stayed and made things right, but I knew, at that moment, I could never,

ever make up for the hurt I had caused this man. I also knew that what I felt for Peter was real and I couldn't deny that, so how could it ever work with Brian again?

#

I also owed it to my kids… yes, I owed it to them to do what I thought was right. I had grown up in a home of unhappy marriages and suffered as a result – I was not about to do that to them. Another vow I made that day, was that my children would know what an amazing father they had – even if he ever did anything to hurt me as he had a right to now, they would never know from me. It has always irked me when I hear parents talking horrendously of the other parent to their children. I swore I would not do this. I hope I fulfilled this promise.

#

Our split was fairly amicable. Brian ensured that the children were well catered for financially and he was one hundred per cent honest about what I was due, even down to his pension which I didn't even think about. Often, in those first few weeks post-discovery, Brian would compliment me, saying things such as, "You were great when you told the children, made it easier for them to hear." However, there was one day when gentle Brian disappeared. I returned from a walk with the dog when he said something I didn't quite hear and I said, 'Pardon?' His response:

#

"I was talking to the dog, not the bitch."

\#

I have to hand it to Brian – he does pull out his one-liners at the appropriate times.

\#

So, there I was, embarking on the third stage of my life. This time though, I was going to be under my own roof, one that belonged to me and where I didn't have to rely on a man to support me. Okay, that is not strictly true. The deposit for the house came from my divorce settlement, the mortgage and bills were paid with money which came from monthly child benefits, tax credits and Brian's child support. But what this did do was give me time – time to do what my grandmother said I couldn't because in her own words, 'I didn't have two planks to rub together' in my head. I finished my college course and embarked on a joint honours degree in History and English. Brian had said to me I was more than capable of getting a degree, but I didn't need to do one as I could always do charity work when the children were grown. However, when I left him, he begged two things of me:

1. Not to tie myself down with another child – I got sterilised as soon as I could because there was absolutely no way I wanted more, and
2. To do my degree, to be independent.

\#

August 20th 2004, I moved into 20 St John's Road. A single mum with four children (I did have Peter, but he didn't live with me) embarking on the most terrifying journey of my life ever. This time though, I knew what I wanted, I knew how to get there, and I knew my own true meaning of love.

The Third Stage

#

There I was, 35 years of age, a divorced mother of four, embarking on, what was to prove, a remarkable journey. That September, Jack started secondary school while Evan was still at pre-school. I managed to juggle my time in college (my degree was through Lampeter University, but all lectures were in Brecon) around the kids and their lives. I hope, at the same time, giving them as normal a life as was possible with a mother who was studying so hard.

#

It took me four years to get my degree, but it was worth it as I gained a 2:1 (my percentage was remarkably close to a first-class degree I think). In the last chapter, I made a passing reference to my grandmother's scathing comment about my lack of intelligence. What she didn't know is that I am, indeed, intelligent, along with the fact that I am an exceptionally hard worker and have a tenacity that is not to be reckoned with. I also want to brag here – I am the only person of my generation in my family to have a degree! My children and my younger brother's eldest daughter are the only ones, so far, to have a degree – both First Class honours. So, Gran, if in some heavenly library you are reading this, you were wrong. Your eldest daughter, the one you were so cruel to as she grew up, produced the academically intelligent branch of the family.

#

Okay, I have always wanted to get that out there officially, and it feels good. Moving on, the year of my PGCE (My Masters level teaching qualification) was the hardest for my kids. I had to leave early in the morning before they went to school, come home after they got home and work nearly every night till late. Rosie and Rhys walked Evan to primary school on their way to High School. Evan stayed in afterschool club and was collected by one of them – occasionally I was able to do this – those times were precious. I want to note my deep gratitude for all four of my kids' sacrifices that year. Their resilience was astounding. Rosie and Evan particularly found this year hard.

#

Evan, because he had never really known what it was like to live with both parents, he had an idealised view of what it might have been. I know now, looking back, that this is where his issues (for want of a better expression) began and if I could turn back the clock, I would do things a little differently. Sometimes, I wonder if my independence was gained to the detriment of my children, but I also know that I was meant to live my life the way I have and can have no regrets for that. I only hope that in reading their mother's narrative (if they do) my children will understand me just a little better and be able to forgive anything I may have done wrong in their eyes. Evan and I are building bridges now and will continue to do so. All he ever needs to know is that I love him, and always will.

#

It was during this year that Rosie's illness was finally diagnosed. When she had started year 7, Rosie was a healthy 8st in weight, but by Christmas, she was 6 1/2. She was having 'accidents' and couldn't eat more than a mouthful or two before feeling full. I took her to the doctors and after several tests, barium meals, etc the results were inconclusive – they had even suggested she might be anorexic, but a psychologist ruled that out early on. In my gut, I knew there was something, but the doctors told me not. I had to accept it, didn't I?

#

I tried, even when Rosie was upset and didn't want to go to school because her tummy was sore, I told her it was probably just coming up to the time when she would get her periods back – they had stopped. Then she had an accident while she was asleep and I was having none of it anymore. I took her to the doctors and demanded they find out what was up. The day we got the IBD diagnosis her doctor cried. He cried in front of us and apologised profusely for not having pushed harder earlier as he should have done. He then arranged for a colonoscopy to confirm whether it was Crohn's or Ulcerative Colitis. In May 2009, I sat writing my final essay for my teaching qualification next to Rosie's hospital bed in Swansea. The surgeon came to confirm that Rosie did indeed have Crohn's disease and put her on a course of steroids.

#

There have been many times when I have wept as I think about this time in Rosie's life. Wept for the pain she suffered and I was unable to do anything about; wept because I somehow feel responsible for her suffering; wept because I'm her mother and that is what mothers do.

#

I have said little about Jack or Rhys and I want to put that straight right now – all my children hold equal and special places in my heart – all for different reasons.

Rosie, because she is my girl. We have shared so many things together both low and high.
Evan, because they are my baby, (Evan is non-binary), they are more like me than they would care to admit. We both enjoy our solitude, we both have very dark and depressive moments, but we both have an ability to pull ourselves out of those moments and heal. I just hope it doesn't take them until they are my age to finally find peace. I have a deep desire to forge deeper ties with my youngest child, and then my peace will be total.

Jack – what can I say about Jack? He is my eldest, my firstborn, my 'little man', (for Jack was always wiser than his years). Recently, Jack shared a memory of his childhood with me. He'd been reading out loud in the kitchen to me while I loaded the dishwasher and he'd put on a silly voice. I turned to look at him and gave him a great big smile. This is a strong memory for Jack and just highlights how simple little things we do naturally as mothers, things that just happen because of our love and connection with our children, can create such warmth in their hearts and stay with them. Jack and I just know each other – I can't put it any other way. He will text me out of the blue and it will be a moment when I really need to hear from him. What I most admire about Jack is his deep loyalty, his strength and his ability to love so fiercely.

#

Jack's partner, my daughter-in-law-in-waiting (he'll hate me for that), is another female in my life who suffers from illness. Lucy is, like Rosie – full of determination to live her life despite her ills and Jack is there right beside her. Jack, of the three boys, is most like his father. This gives me an inner faith that he will be there for Lucy no matter what.

#

Rhys – so different and yet so similar to his siblings. When I completed my teacher training, Peter and I (by this time engaged to be married) decided to move in together and moved to England. In the time we lived in West Sussex, Rhys made some very close friendships which he holds to this day. Rhys has a very sharp wit. He can cut you down with his tongue faster than any guillotine. But, and it is a big but, his sharpness is embedded in an utter and total sense of what is right. His morality is so strong that I would challenge anyone to find an issue with his reasoning for all that he does and all that he has.

#

After a few years in England, Peter and I decided to move to Scotland (more on that in the next chapter). Jack had stayed with his father when we moved to England; Rosie was married to Fred; Evan decided to move back to Wales to live with their dad and Rhys moved to Scotland with us.

We have been in Scotland for five years now and in that time, Rhys saved up for his own place and has now been living there for nearly two years. My bond with Rhys, always strong, has grown much more so in these last few years. As mentioned, it was Rhys who bought me the 'Book of Obscure Sorrows', or, more accurately, bought it for himself, read it, loved it and knew I would, so gave it to me for my birthday – see, he always has to be honest. Rhys, like Evan and I, enjoy our solitude. Rhys just likes it much more. He can come across as reclusive and almost off-hand, but I know my son. He is a man who would do anything for anyone who needed his help and loves his family deeply, but mostly, he is his own person.

#

With regards to my children, it is my hope that my past, which led to my determination, means that they will have the opportunity to become their own people, and it has not left their lives short of what might otherwise have been. Without my past, I would never have met their father and fallen in love, and I would not have had them. I am glad that my past happened as it did, as it led me to Brian and therefore the existence of my children, and no other reason. That does not mean that I wish it had never happened, just that I have accepted that it did and here I am now.

Now

\#

At last, I come to the final part of my narrative to date. For this, I shall start in 2009, an eventful year for many reasons:

\#

- First Rosie's diagnosis,
- I began my first-ever teaching post at Wildern School in Southampton,
- Peter arranged our wedding secretly of which he informed me by text,
- Rosie had an emergency operation to save her life, which left her with a colostomy bag,
- Peter and I were married, despite snow which tried to stop us from getting to Scotland.

\#

Following the diagnosis in May, Rosie's health did not improve. During an exploratory colonoscopy in December of that year, it was discovered that her Crohn's had caused extensive damage and that she would need to be prepared mentally for having a temporary colostomy bag. We didn't get time to prepare her. Her bowel had been perforated in the May, been covered by the damaged bowel in the meantime and only been exposed during this operation.

It meant that she needed an 8-hour emergency surgery to remove 18 inches of her bowel and fit her bag. Rosie took it in her stride. I was with her every step of the way. I was at every appointment and by her bed every moment. I would have been nowhere else. When she was in surgery, I was accompanied in my waiting by the Boss – 'Drive All Night' on repeat. Rosie's colostomy was reversed the following year and again, 'Drive All Night' kept me company through the six-hour operation.

#

During this time, I was in my NQT year at Wildern – they were amazing. Most NQTs who were absent as much as I was would not pass their year and would not make it further in teaching. However, with their support – allowing Rosie to spend time at school so that I could feed her through the NG tube and still be at work, not deducting pay when I was with her in the hospital (in the head's own words, the time I took off because of Rosie was exceptional – I was not a shirker and should not be punished for being a mother), I made it – with flying colours I might add. Mary-Lou Litten will always be the head teacher I will most admire. Her management is second to none. There is no one in my eyes who could ever replace her in that capacity.

#

For two reasons, the wedding nearly didn't happen. First and foremost, if Rosie was not up to going to her father's for Christmas, or travelling up to Scotland with us, it would be postponed. Secondly, the snow. The flight was delayed, cancelled, delayed, back on again, cancelled again and finally after many hours, we actually took off. My only regret about that day was the necessity to keep it from our children. It was always going to be a difficult day for the children, none more so than for my stepsons Michael and George. Therefore, it was just easier to go ahead and do it. It had been Peter's intention that we would go, have my mum and dad as witnesses and that would be it – I would have been more than happy with that.

#

In the end, Mum went full throttle and arranged a meal and an evening party. It was a great day (albeit tinged with sadness that the six kids were absent). However, the best part about the day was my dad's face. He got to 'give me away' – I had only ever seen the look of pride on his face when he watched Frank's success as a footballer. Now, it was there for me, correction for us. Mum too that day – her joy at witnessing my marriage was plain for all to see.

#

Fast forward to another important year – 2012. This was the year I started my second teaching post at Westgate, later to become Ormiston Six Villages Academy (OSVA). More importantly, the year my mother finally married the one man who could make her happy – Alec. What a man! Not just in physical stature but also in his ability to put up with my mum's foibles. The day they got married, I burst with pride when Alec asked me to stand up and make a speech. All I could say was that Alec was more than welcome in our family, that I was grateful to him because he was perfect and he was perfect because he loved my mum.

#

My time at OSVA was bittersweet. I had learned so much in the three years I'd worked at Wildern and brought much of this to my job at OSVA. I ended up being the Deputy Head of English there and absolutely loved my job. But this was all marred by the bullying nature of a new headteacher (I will not name her – not for any Harry Potter(esq) reason but because she doesn't deserve to be recognised in that way in my narrative). This woman and her management approach scarred me. When I left OSVA I was not a confident teacher, I was no longer the strong, capable professional who had arrived from Wildern. In short, professionally, I was a slim picture of my former self. For this reason, the high cost of living where we were located and my dad's failing health, led us to the decision to move to Scotland in 2017. Another decision that was not taken lightly. It meant leaving Rosie behind and losing Evan to Wales, but it was the natural thing to do. So, I went on a job hunt and at the third time of asking, was successful. Importantly, for my professional self, it was the only interview where I had to deliver a lesson, and it was the lesson (judged by the Deputy as the best she had ever seen) that got me the job.

So, there I was, April 2017, starting a new job and living with Dad (while Peter and Rhys stayed south to sell the house). Those few months I had with Dad were so precious – hilarious and sad, but very precious. He was, by this time, well into his Dementia diagnosis. There were nights when I would sneak into his room to switch off his hearing aid, just to have him jump out of bed fully clothed and ready to take me on a trip to the seaside. Mornings, when I would wake up to him in my room asking why I wasn't up and ready for school – it took me a while to realise he meant me as a student, not a teacher! One prevailing memory is our walks into town. There is a particular part of that walk where the buildings open up and you can see the sea. At this point, Dad's memory would always be jogged regarding something or other. I'd heard it so often that I'd forgotten. What sticks though is that I never, ever reminded him that I'd heard it before. I always treated everything he said as if it was the first time. The first time I replied with, 'aha', he immediately did an Elvis impersonation. From then on, I always replied with 'aha' and he always responded the same way. Dad was mad about Elvis.

#

Dad passed from this world on 28th November 2019. Frank and I had taken it in turns to make sure he was not alone over the course of the proceeding week as we had made the decision to stop treatment because of his quality-of-life outcome. At 7.45 p.m. that night, Dad took his last breath. I was by his side. Now, my mum left Dad when I was nearly 12, but it was Frank who was Dad's natural child and it was Frank who had grown up with him fully. My heart ached in that moment for two reasons; the passing of the man I knew as Dad and my younger brother Frank. He should have been the one there, not me.

#

Move forward to 1st January 2021 and I was in the same position again, but this time with Alec. Again, it was 7.45 p.m. when he took his last breath and it was me that was with him (Frank had been with him all day, I just took over to let him go home for a rest). The situation was identical – both men were 4 months away from their 80th birthday, and both died at 7.45 p.m. with me by their side. Again, my heart ached – ached for the passing of Alec, a man who made my mother whole, and for my mother who couldn't be there because she was at home desperately ill with Covid – the killer that took Alec from us. Later, my mum was to tell me she thought that the reason I was the one with them, was because there was something in me that made it possible for them to pass. My brother, well, he calls me the 'Grim Reaper'. I still love him though!

#

I have made very little mention of my older brother Rob – I don't know why, but I do know he has always had my back, has always supported me and I have always felt guilt (still do) at lying all those years ago. Now, Rob is leaving us. He has a diagnosis of early-onset dementia due to head trauma and is no longer the person he once was. I have not seen him for a while. Mum visits him and says he doesn't want us to see him the way he is. My plan is to wait until he is in a condition where he will no longer know that I am who I am and go to England to see him. What I do want on record is this: Rob suffered throughout his life, following a horrendous accident as a child which left him scarred and blind in one eye, he was bullied mercilessly. Despite all that, Rob went on to have a reasonable life and he does not deserve to be the way he is now. Rob, you will always be my protective big brother, brave and strong (stupid at times) and always funny. I love you.

Epilogue

\#

I began this in 2019 with the statement made by Peter about genetics. I end this now in April 2023 and like its inception, it shall end with Peter.

\#

In all my years since leaving The Lord Palmerston and the abuse behind, I have had the love of two good men. Brian loved me, I loved him and I grew as a person with him. Then came Peter. With Peter, I have found the strength and courage to become the real me. He has loved me fully (not that Brian didn't). He has given me the space I needed to realise my dream of becoming a teacher. He has sat and listened while I cried at the demise of my childhood and encouraged me to get therapy.

\#

I did this, before my most recent, current and final therapy. I undertook Cognitive Behaviour Therapy which helped. I had 'normal' therapy where I was told I would only get better if I told my mum what really happened (well if you read this now Mum, you'll definitely know). Most importantly, Peter was there. He never told me I had to 'get over it', and never made light of my experiences.

#

I can honestly say, now that I am writing the final few words of my narrative, I am at peace. A peace I never, ever thought I could attain. Thank you, Peter, for giving me the strength to write this, to acknowledge that my truth was just that – my truth. That it doesn't matter how anyone else views it – it was my experience and by putting it down and sharing, it would help. It has. I love you.

* * *